INTIMATE PORTRAITS

INTIMATE PORTRAITS

Being Recollections of

Maxim Gorky
John Galsworthy
Edward Sheldon
George Moore
Sidney Howard
& Others

By

BARRETT H. CLARK

KENNIKAT PRESS
Port Washington, N. Y./London

Manufactured by Taylor Publishing Company   Dallas, Texas

ESSAY AND GENERAL LITERATURE INDEX REPRINT SERIES

To

WILLIAM SLOANE

who liked something about
these papers and encouraged me
to think that others might
find them worth reading.

CONTENTS

PREFACE

BY WAY OF PREFACE

THE six papers that make up this book are offered largely in the hope that the men who are their subjects may prove as appealing to the reader as they were to me before I had any intention of writing about them for publication. While it was only natural, my profession and basic interests being what they are, that plays and the theater should be so often mentioned in the pages that follow, my chief interest lay in trying to bring some semblance of life to certain men I had had a chance to study and observe at first-hand. My aim was, without too much critical comment, to permit each to do and say as much that was characteristic as I had been able to retain in my memory; to allow each to reveal himself as naturally and completely as possible within the means at my command.

I have taken some pains to let each act his part as he had done in that period, or in those periods, when I was, as it were, a private spectator at his performance. No one, of course, can report such things dispassionately and with complete scientific detachment; but so far as that kind of reporting was possible to me, I have tried to be an accurate and faithful reporter. I believe that in offering all the available evidence on a man's character a reporter is more likely to present some sort of recognizable biographical likeness than he could do by trying to interpret the meaning of the evidence, omitting what seems to him irrelevant or trivial, and depending on the imagination to supply what is actually missing, or may have escaped the eye or ear of the observer. I think that too often the reporter is unable to decide just what evidence may be illuminating to others, and what may not, and that the wise course for him is to tell all he has learned through actual observation. Naturally, what he sees can be only a small part of the ultimate truth, whatever that may turn out to be, but if he can add his own bit to the potential sum-total, he may perhaps serve some useful purpose in helping someone else construct a more elaborate and all-embracing biography, if that should be called for later on. But no one can say what man may deserve an exhaustive biography fifty years in the future, and many a tentative and fragmentary portrait, like those in this volume, will remain as isolated documents. I am publishing these papers not so much to furnish biographical data that may appeal to those who are interested in a particular *literary* figure, but because what I have found of human interest may prove to be more important and lasting than what the man happens to have accomplished. I believe that man himself is likely to remain for a long time the proper subject of study that Pope declared him to be more than two centuries ago. By way of illustrating this belief I have added to the other five subjects here, all men whose artistic accomplishments are well-known, a sixth. The last figure in my collection is that of a man not known to fame, whose accomplishments are familiar to only a relatively few persons, whose incidental writings are of little or no consequence, and whose gift to the world lay simply in the richness of his personal contacts with others. The fragmentary notes on "Carl B. Clinton," which is not his real name, will I hope persuade the reader that even if he had been famous as a painter or poet he would have been no more deserving of a portrait than he is now.

The paper on George Moore comes closest to my ideas, as above outlined, on one way to write biography. This is the longest in the book, and most of the conversations reported I set down within a few hours of the time I heard them. Boswell did the same kind of thing, and I can claim no more than that I have tried, in my own small way, to follow in a way the methods of the Master. The shorter portrait of Gorky is likewise an attempt at on-the-spot reporting, though many of the writer's statements I have checked with Gorky's secretary and one other person who knew him at the time I did. This was all the more necessary because some of our long talks, when Gorky spoke only Russian and I mostly English (and of course no Russian), as recorded in my sketchy notes, needed clarification and correction. The Sidney Howard letters required occasional commentary, and that I have supplied entirely from memory. The Sheldon paper, written long after I had seen the playwright for the last time, I composed entirely from memory. I made a pretty accurate record of the visit of the Galsworthys at the time, and I have used these notes in preparing the present paper. "Carl B. Clinton" was written only a few weeks before the manuscript of this book was sent to the printer. I had no written records of any kind, and the portrait is therefore more in the nature of a mood piece, a fragmentary, somewhat impressionistic series of short recollections in which the actual dates and occurrences, while substantially accurate, are somewhat mixed up: what may have happened in the spring of 1913 in London I have not hesitated to set down for the winter of 1910 in Paris if that served my purpose. The actual words of the speaker as I report them are, I am convinced, truer in spirit to what he said than if I had been able to depend on contemporary notes.

A short section from the *George Moore* was first published in the *American Mercury*. Half a dozen parts of the entire manuscript were used in Joseph M. Hone's *Life of George Moore*. A good deal of the *Maxim Gorky* originally appeared in *The Nineteenth Century* (of London), and some of it in *The Stratford Journal* (of Boston). A small part of the *John Galsworthy* was published in the book section of the *New York Sunday Sun*. Some of the Howard letters appeared in one issue of *Theater Arts Monthly,* and others in *Theater Arts,* successor to the Monthly. The *Edward Sheldon* in its original form was read on Pipe Night some years ago at the Players' Club in New York. Everything that has been published heretofore, as well as the Sheldon paper, has been revised.

The Sidney Howard letters are here printed by permission of the writer's widow, Leopoldine Damrosch Howard.

B.H.C.

INTIMATE PORTRAITS

MAXIM GORKY
THE HAPPY EXILE

MAXIM GORKY

I HAD tried twice to get in touch with Maxim Gorky in the late autumn of 1922 when I was living in Berlin, but my newspaper friends said it was no use: they had tried, and got nowhere, and besides, the writer was dying, and wouldn't talk for publication even if I were lucky enough to get an interview. But I decided to write a letter, and I got genial and friendly Louis Lochner to back it up with a statement that I was not particularly interested in politics and would keep off the subject if I were asked to do so. On January 8, 1923, I received a short note from Marie Budberg, Gorky's secretary, saying that "Mr. Gorky will be very pleased to see you next Friday or Saturday."

Saarow is a small town fifty miles east of Berlin, with a spick-and-span new-looking square which opens out before you as you step from the villa-like railroad station. Bleak it looked as I got off the train on that dark winter afternoon and walked, against a stinging wind, to the sanatorium in the pine-woods where Gorky was living. Why, I wondered, had I come out here to see the old lion in exile, perhaps even on his death-bed? I had agreed to avoid discussing politics, but after all, what had I to say, or ask, that could excuse this intrusion on the famous invalid? I was nervous, wished I had never come; but I *was* expected, and I must see it through. The small stucco building I had been directed to looked a little forbidding as I came up to it, and I began to invent important-sounding questions to ask. After all, I had come fifty miles for this visit, and I was afraid I might look like an impertinent fool. I hoped for a second that Gorky was out, or had gone away, but the nurse at the door ushered me in at once, and shouted upstairs to announce that a caller was in the waiting-room; would Herr Gorky walk down, or should the visitor come up to him?

A woman's voice invited me to come right up. At the top of the stairs stood Marie Budberg, the charming and unusually capable woman who—as I soon learned—had taken over the management of the writer's affairs. As she was showing me into the living-room, Gorky himself rose from a wicker arm-chair in a corner. I don't know how tall he is, but he looked well over six feet. He chuckled, and gurgled, and clucked, burst into smiles, and embraced me. Then he pushed me into the most comfortable chair in the room, and began talking Russian at a great rate.

"Mr. Gorky," said Mme. Budberg, "speaks only Russian, so I'll have to interpret for you." This was disappointing; I had expected he would know a little French or German, or possibly English. "He says he never thought it worth-while learning any language but his own, since all the great books are so well translated into Russian." Evidently he understood what was being said, because he muttered, again with smiles and gesticulations, a dozen names, which I could easily make out as "Shakespeare," "Homer," "Cervantes," and "Balzac."

Preparations were at once made for tea. Mme. Budberg hurried out of the room, and Gorky and I were left alone. He stood most of the while, and paced up and down between the small desk and the window. How tall he is! Narrow shoulders and chest; deep furrows down the cheeks; a broad peasant's nose, wide mouth, and the youngest light-blue eyes I had ever seen in a grown man. The thick bushy hair of the early pictures is gone; it is short, cropped, brushed back, with a low, stiff military pompadour starting beyond the slightly receding forehead. I imagined I could see some traces of suffering on this expressive face, but the constant smile makes it hard to think that this jovial fellow ever had a serious worry. The drooping moustache might add dignity to his appearance if it weren't that he gives the impression of wearing it as though it were theatrical make-up.

He wears a thick gray sweater-vest, a blue shirt with soft collar, gray baggy trousers, and large heavy walking-boots.

Before I know it, I find myself chatting away in English and listening to Gorky in Russian, just as though each of us understood what the other said. But, strangely, after a few minutes we did manage to understand. Then Mme. Budberg comes in, and we settle down to tea. She smiles understandingly as I tell her how easily we had got along without her. At this time, and on all my later visits, I hardly knew whether we spoke through an interpreter or not. Gorky is so wholly and unreflectively—almost childishly—eager to put over what he has to say that language barriers just don't exist. All thought of the man's past, as literary man and revolutionist, is obliterated for me the moment he opens his mouth. He is wholly without conscious dignity, and whatever interests him wholly absorbs his attention.

Occasionally Mme. Budberg helps us out, but oftener than not he sweeps her aside with a wide gesture, and coming close to me, sits on the arm of my chair or plumps himself on the floor in front of me, laughing, spluttering, gesticulating— and usually making his meaning clear. Then I begin doing the same thing, and the system works!

After the quick ceremony of tea, the tea things are carried out, and Gorky chatters about books. The room is lined with them, the closets stuffed full, they lie in heaps on desk and floor. Spread open on a chair is *The Last of the Mohicans*, a Russian translation for which Gorky wrote the preface.

"What do you think of Cooper? Do you Americans still read him or do you consider him old-fashioned? He's one of my favorite writers. Which of his stories do you like best? *I* love them all. Are they authentic pictures of pioneer life?"

Ah, and here is a series of war memoirs, just in from the publisher. "Do you like such things? I'm bored to death by them, aren't you? There are six volumes already written by some general, and so far he's only reached the beginning of 1917. How many more are coming? Brrr!"

And he stalks across the room to indicate with his finger a spot at the end of the bookcase. He roars with laughter as he returns to my chair, ready to hear me laugh with him. It's a little embarrassing at first—but not to Gorky.

It amuses me—and Gorky—to recall this first visit in January. Though he had made it clear that he simply would not talk politics, I had taken the trouble beforehand to read his latest collection of political essays. I was a bit troubled by the man's militant attitude toward certain ideas and institutions, and I was afraid that his "Russian gloom" would cast a shadow over my visit. When I confessed this next time I went to Saarow, Gorky burst into one of those torrential laughs that I was later to get used to, and said he didn't think I cared any more about politics than he did. Now did I, really?

"Books are the only things worth talking about, don't you agree?"

No matter what we start discussing, the talk always gets back to books and authors. When I saw that his veto on politics came rather from fear of boredom than from getting into trouble, I tried occasionally to lead him into a discussion on Russia, political prisoners, Lenin, free speech.

"No, no," he said when I asked him what else he intended to do in the field of political writing, "I'm a very bad controversialist. Take that book you brought with you to-day—*The Destruction of Personality*—you don't really like it, do you? I don't look well in the role of political commentator. Let me give you a nice book!" And he trotted to the bookcase and pulled out a copy of the German translation of the second volume of his autobiography, *Among Strange Men*. "You'll like this. I hope you can read it. *I* can't."

Mme. Budberg, ever-watchful, tactful, quiet, interrupts a long discussion on Dostoievsky, and reminds us that dinner is ready.

"No, no!," and he waves her aside. "We're having carrots—I can smell them—yes, I know they're good for me, but
I loathe them! *You'd* rather talk books, wouldn't you?" This,
of course, to me. And we talk on. Then a whisper to me from
Mme. Budberg, and Gorky, with a burst of laughter, gives
in. "Maybe *you* are hungry?" he asks. "Do you hate carrots,
too?"

We dined in a small private room, regularly reserved for
Gorky and his "party"; Gorky's young son Pyeshkov and his
pretty wife, a Doctor Kaplun, Mme. Budberg, a young French
writer, and two or three others—not to mention two cats and
a dog; these made a merry chattering group. As I looked
round the table I wondered what had brought these people
together at this remote spot on the plains of Prussia, and I
learned, in the intervals between outbursts of laughter, how
Gorky's son had recently married and being without a job
had attached himself and his wife to the little group of refu-
gees; the others, I gathered, were living chiefly on the meager
funds Gorky was able to collect from the sale of articles and
fiction. Mme. Budberg seemed the only one who was actually
working—and contributing more than her share.

The second Gorky is through eating he draws an immense napkin from his belt, and throwing it on the table,
comes round to my chair and lifts me up out of it. "Come back
to my room now. We've had no chance to do any real talking yet. Come along!"

And back we go, Mme. Budberg with us. Gorky lights a
cigarette, sticks it in a long bone holder and drapes himself
over the corner of a sofa.

"Now," he announces, "you're going to tell me what
you're doing in your country. Who are the new writers? Have
you a national drama of your own yet? What do you think of
Upton Sinclair's latest novel? And tell me everything you
know about this O'Neill playwriting fellow."

And I begin to tell something about Willa Cather,
O'Neill, Sinclair Lewis and Dreiser. Gorky begins to fidget.

"Yes, yes, go ahead! Tell me more. These books you tell about should be translated. Your O'Neill friend sounds interesting, but maybe a little bit too—Russian, shall I say? But he has guts, I imagine, from what you tell me of his work. If he's as good as you say his plays will soon be translated and produced all over Russia."

A quick interchange of questions with Mme. Budberg, who nods to him; then she turns to me:

"Mr. Gorky says you shouldn't thank *him* for being allowed to come out here. He wants to make use of you!" (Gorky chuckles at this and rubs his hands together). "He's starting a new magazine, *Besseda*, an international quarterly. It's to be published in Russian. Romain Rolland has just sent him an article on Ghandi, and he asks will you write something on America? Nothing technical—just your own frank opinions—something on the theater—"

"Teatr! Teatr! O'Neill!" mutters Gorky, smiling and nodding.

"You will be the first to write an article on O'Neill in Russian—"

"O. Henry, too"—and he pronounces this "O. Chenry" (the *Ch* as in German): there is no H in Russian.

"Mr. Gorky is a tremendous admirer of O. Henry, and wants an article on him. Will you write it?"

I will try, at any rate. I shall be paid, I'm told, but in German money. It won't amount to much, maybe a dollar, just what the other writers get. Now, I know that Gorky has very little money himself, and I offer to do the articles without payment, but he rises and strides over to me with a scowl:

"We all write for money—and you shall have your pay like the rest of us. Let's hear no more about doing this work for nothing. Understood?"

"And now, Mr. Gorky, if you don't mind, I'd like to ask *you* a few questions." I want to know what he thinks about his own plays, especially *The Lower Depths*. I had seen productions of this in English, French, German, and in Russian during the past season. I had no special question I wanted answered, but I was anxious to hear what he had to say about playwriting in general. He wanders over again from his place by the window, and stands impatiently between Mme. Budberg and me, interrupting every moment or two, like a child being discussed by his elders.

"What does he say? What does he want to know? Oh, my plays!" A gesture of disgust, a wry smile, and a grunt. "I don't like my plays. Tell him I don't like them at all. Let's not talk about them."

But I did want to know. Personally, I preferred his novels and stories, but he must have had some special reason for trying his hand at the dramatic form. *The Lower Depths*, above all others, had proved throughout Europe and even in the English-speaking countries, that it had a universal appeal.

"Possibly," he admits. "Perhaps. But when I wrote that play I knew nothing about the theater. The thing just came out of me, and fell on to the paper. Matter of fact, all my plays are bad—very bad. I don't like them. I don't even want to think of them any more. But—wait a moment, I have a new play, and maybe it's not so bad as the others. It is called *The Old Man*. I have the manuscript somewhere around. Look in the bathroom there—I think I left it—Never mind, it's somewhere else. I think it has some good things in it. It was written only a few years ago. Produced in Russia. No, it's not published, but I'll have Mme. Budberg make a literal translation for you; you can revise the English and have it acted in your country. Or, if you don't like it, feed it to the fishes, if they want it."

"Why do you think it better than your other plays?"

"It's the idea that interests me, and I think its theme might appeal to Americans. It's the story of a Siberian exile, an ex-convict who after terrible struggles has succeeded in building up a fine business of his own. But there is another man who knows his secret and holds it over him; he gradually manages to ruin the ex-convict's life."

"That sounds different from your other plays; much simpler; surely there is more to it than that?"

"A good deal, but we'll come to that later. What pleases me is that it's more theatrical than anything else I've done. It's—"

He jumps up and begins pulling papers from his desk.

"Here we are—I have it." And he begins reading a speech, then stops and smiles. "You ought to learn Russian, young man!"

"Let me interrupt a moment, please, and ask what made you write this particular story in play form?"

"The source of all art," he announces, "is no more than the overflow of the—shall we say, soul?—it oozes out into various impressions of life. When the artist can no longer contain himself he simply produces his works of art. What precise form these will take is a matter of small importance. Sometimes it's a play, sometimes a novel, sometimes a picture or a symphony. If what I have written has taken the form of plays, that was because it had to be that way—I was impelled to bring them forth all dressed up for the theater."

"But a play," I interrupt, "is a highly specialized form, for which the writer must have some practical knowledge of the technical processes. Did you ever actually *study* the form?"

"Never," he explodes, with an immense guffaw. "That is probably why my plays are so bad." Then, with a grave smile, "but maybe they would have been worse if I'd read Freytag and the others. But to come back to your question: I *did* try *The Old Man* first as a story, but it wouldn't come that way: it just wrote itself as a play. The idea wouldn't express itself in narrative form."

"You began to tell me the idea, but I started you off in another direction."

"The idea is quite simple, and very un-Russian. It is that

(10)

suffering gives no one the right to judge the world. The world is not bad, and if it seems so to some of us we have only ourselves to blame; it is we who are bad. The world, indeed, is good. It is a happy world; what is wrong is that we human beings never seem happy unless we are creating misery for ourselves. If the world were evil and man the victim of a malevolent fate, we should all go hang ourselves; but we go on living, building, creating, enjoying ourselves, following our trades and professions, and always hoping. We continue to hope because this world is basically right, and life is sweet in spite of everything; we know, without asking for proof, that this is so. The man who complains of his suffering is utterly selfish; he makes suffering his chief occupation, and glories in it. How can such a man help being miserable? He has only himself to blame."

Strange words, these! I try to recall among all the works of this man some story or play that exemplifies the idea, but I can think of none.

"What bothers you?" he asks, and I tell him:

"You are going to lose your reputation as a Russian writer; even Russian comedies have an undercurrent of bitterness."

"That is no longer true. Take *The Old Man*, it marks a new departure, a revolt against 'Russian Gloom'. It shows that the human will is an active and potent thing. The play is a denial of the devastating philosophy of Sanin. It proclaims the strength of the individual. You will soon discover that Russia is neither wholly pessimistic nor abnormally cynical. Suffering and madness and death are not the only subjects we can write about.

"When I am ill I hate myself. For my past sufferings I have only myself to blame; have I a right to shift responsibility to the shoulders of my fellowmen or to that poor overworked abstraction we cowards call Fate? I have been in prison; I've been mercilessly beaten, I have nearly starved to death. All, all my own fault! It was my business to avoid such troubles. I have no complaint against my fellowmen, against 'society', or against the world.

"And now, perhaps," he goes on, "you will understand what I have written about Dostoievsky and Tolstoy. Gigantic writers, both of them, but their influence has been bad. The philosophy of despair that colors most Russian literature since their day is due largely to them. Both preached the subjection of the will—or denied the will altogether—and almost succeeded in destroying our faith and initiative."

"But why," I ask, "do you blame these writers for failing to live up to certain standards that have nothing to do with the art they practice? You surely don't believe that the writer of fiction should make it his business to teach moral or social doctrines?"

"Not at all, and to make myself clear let me take two examples—Flaubert and Tolstoy. Both are first-rate artists—granted. Now with Flaubert's ideas I have no quarrel: Flaubert deliberately stood aloof from politics and ideas. But Tolstoy is another matter; like Dostoievsky, he made definite claims to leadership, he was confessedly a preacher and reformer. Both proclaimed themselves representatives of social, religious, and intellectual movements; it is as leaders, not as artists, that I attack them. Don't you see?"

"But what actual harm have they done?"

"Tolstoy and Dostoievsky were in agreement at one period. That was in the 80's, during the reaction under Alexander III. At almost the same moment these tremendously influential thinkers helped the forces of conservatism by playing into the hands of the enemies of freedom and tolerance. Said Dostoievsky, 'Bend your pride, and be patient'; said Tolstoy, 'Wait: do not oppose evil with evil'. As if there were any other way to do it! Since that time most of our writers and thinkers have succumbed to the philosophy of despair, and this naturally finds its reflection in much of our writing. The will has been weakened, and pessimism has taken its place."

He sits silent a moment, blowing smoke at the ceiling. I take out my English translation of his *Reminiscences of Tolstoy*, and we glance through it together. These random notes, I tell him, have given us glimpses of Tolstoy the human being that made the Master somewhat less repellent than I imagined him to have been. I want to ask certain questions, but Gorky smiles and shuts the book.

"I wish someone would write about *me!*" A loud burst of laughter. At the time I couldn't quite understand why he said this, but as I got to know him better, I saw that it was one of his little jokes. The idea of anyone's troubling to write *him* up—! In the Tolstoy book I tell him he has written illuminatingly about himself. He reports, for instance, the older writer as saying to him, "You're a very remarkable creature . . . it is as if you sprang into life full-grown."

That was strange, unless "full-grown" means young, for I can't imagine his ever having been anything but young.

We must have talked late that night. I find many casual notes hurriedly scratched in my account book on the trip back to Berlin, some of them now entirely meaningless: we jumped from one subject to another. I knew I couldn't recall everything.

"How old is this man?" That is in one corner of a page in my book. "Sixty?" Perhaps. Is he really an invalid? I can't say. Probably. But he behaves like no invalid I ever saw. . . .

Here is another note, longer than most, in answer to a question on Tolstoy's *What Is Art?*

"It's a sincere book," was the answer. "Tolstoy was always sincere. He believed everything he wrote, though he was often uncertain about his convictions before or after he formulated them, even his religious convictions. A born preacher. He used to remind me of our popular Russian folk-figure, Vassika Buslayeff, who is always experimenting, searching, doing what he oughtn't to do, getting into all sorts of scrapes, just to see what would happen.

"He had a perverse streak; he liked to do and say things that astonished people, and that's one of the reasons he wrote *What Is Art?* A strange book—the result of a passing mood. The queerest thing about it is that Tolstoy (I hardly like to say it, but it's true) was very ignorant of his facts. He just didn't know the history of art. The worst fallacy in his reasoning was that all culture is based on religion, art, and science; he tried to eliminate art, which is one of the most important elements. You can't tear out the keystone and have any real culture left.

"Yes, Tolstoy was a curious mixture. He was always declaring, for instance, that books were of small importance in life; he would make fun of me, calling me a 'bookman'. But, let me tell you, I used to read to him, sometimes from my own unpublished work, and occasionally from others' work. He was often moved and interested. Once I read some passage out of Lamennais, and the tears rolled down his cheeks.

"Books mean more and more to me the older I grow. When I was in the cabinet under Lenin, I began editing a huge series of world classics." He went to the bookcase and tumbled into my lap a score of paper-bound booklets. "See here, we planned to issue four thousand different titles, each printing a hundred thousand copies. We only brought out about a hundred titles; manufacturing costs were too high at the time. But the idea *will* be worked out some day. Lectures, newspapers, motion pictures, plays—these are all very well, but books are better. Think of it, to-day you can sell a hundred thousand copies of a classic in starving Russia!" . . .

Here are the names of America's authors that are widely read to-day, and a few of Gorky's comments:

"Upton Sinclair, of course. We read him for his ideas. His books are scarcely 'literature', but the ideas appeal to us. There's O. Henry, too, and Bret Harte—both great favorites. And Mark Twain, Howells, James, Horace Traubel, Le Roy

Scott, Jack London, Ambrose Bierce. And your classics are our classics: Thoreau, Poe, Whitman, Emerson, Cooper."

I had asked particularly about Jack London. Surely it was his Socialism that interested Russian readers?

"Oh, no. His popularity with us is an encouraging sign. He has been tremendously influential. He had a lot to do with our current literary movement. You don't know our new writers yet, but you will, and you won't recognize the old Russia. The best of the new men no longer worship the god of despair; they have begun to exalt the will. That, I think, is largely due to London. One of our most gifted young poets has sounded a new note. He's a real talent—his name's Khodassevitch. His writings have become a kind of new gospel to us, a gospel never before heard on the lips of any Russian writer:

> Sing not the praises of the conqueror,
> Nor pity the conquered.

The conqueror needs no praise, you understand, and the conquered no comfort. We young Russians have no love of suffering! It is a happy world."

Just after I wrote these words down I turned to a short passage in the Gorky-Tolstoy book, and found this—Tolstoy speaking to Gorky:

"You are funny—don't be offended, but you are funny. It's remarkable you are so good-natured, you who have had such excellent reasons for being full of hatred. Yes, you have good reason to hate. . . . Though I don't understand your soul —it's very subtle—but your heart is clear."

. . . . . .

It was some weeks before I went out to Saarow again. I wrote one of the articles I had promised him, and Gorky read it in translation. He thanked me, and the next day took it to the printer in Berlin, but he sent me word that he hoped I wouldn't mind the shortened form of my name; it would have to appear without the middle initial, since there was no H in Russian. He thought this a grand joke on me.

Marie Budberg meantime called on my wife and me at our rooms in Berlin, to deliver her rough literal version of *The Old Man,* which now bore the new title of *The Judge.*

My next two or three visits with Gorky are fixed clearly in mind, but most of the notes I took (until I went to Freiburg in the fall) are less detailed.

I see I spent a day at Saarow in May, and lunched at the Sanatorium with the entire "Gorky colony."

I was told about Frank Harris, who had come out to see Gorky a few days before, and after a short conversation, was told to leave. The first question he asked was why Gorky had left the details of his early sex life out of his autobiography, and Gorky had asked Harris if he had come all the way from Berlin to find that out? Thereupon Harris had started to tell Gorky what an important fellow he was in England and America, and Gorky had got up and left the room.

Gorky turned to me and said he knew Harris by reputation, but preferred to let Harris think he didn't.

After lunch Gorky, his son and daughter-in-law, Marie Budberg, and two dogs and I went for a long walk by the shores of a small lake. We had tea at a cafe, and (according to my notes) "discussed humor—its nationality—its civilizing influence. We exchanged samples, and strangely enough Gorky recognized the point in most of my jokes. I showed him, in a magazine, a typical Amercian satire on a Russian play, and he roared as it was translated to him. He prefers, he says, the broad joke —the more obvious and clownish varieties of humor. Exaggeration, he claimed, was a revealing form of truth. Most Russian humor is rooted in the peasant: it is obvious, pointed, physical, often cruel. Most other forms of humor in Russia are only importations. The genuine article there is akin to British humor: that of the Elizabethans, of Smollett and Dickens.

He spoke of the Kamerny Theater, which had recently come to Berlin. "That's what I mean. Those fellows are returning to the natural sources of real humor."

On our way back he illustrated his theory, and made puns about the name-plates on the door-posts along the street. Some of these must have been amusingly indecent; while everyone laughed, Mme. Budberg refused to explain the points. She prided herself, I think, on being a trifle less "Russian" than the others.

We circled round the village, and came back to the lake again. Gorky wanted to go rowing, but all the boats were in use. "He looked at the fish, coming to the surface—stood there watching and making comments for twenty minutes. Everything, anything, seems to interest him, to absorb all his attention. He starts to tell something 'extraordinary,' and most of the time it turns out to be almost pointless. For example, 'The most amazing thing: I saw a little woman yesterday at the fruit-shop. She was dressed from head to foot in green. Everything —shoes, hat, gloves—green, so green!' "

Our walk had no particular objective; it was a leisurely excursion. Gorky would stop and look at a cloud, a squirrel, a mangy dog, an old man, the plaster peeling from the walls of a summer villa. He impressed me as one who has just recovered his eyesight after years of blindness, or as one who has just been born—with all his faculties—into a world he has heard much about but had never seen. His comments show a mental virginity that is astounding in an adult.

And he never seemed to get tired. Yet on our return to the Sanatorium Mme. Budberg made him lie down, while she and I began work on *The Old Man*. There were all sorts of questions I wanted answered: I was putting the crude translation into form for publication, and there were sentences and passages I was not sure about.

We had not been at this five minutes before the door opened, and Gorky stood looking at us, dressed in a faded blue Japanese wrapper, looking like some character in *The Mikado*.

I glanced up from the manuscript, but Mme. Budberg had heard the intruder, and with a quick gesture and a word ordered him back to his room. He raised one hand high above his head, crossed himself, winked at me, and left us.

"He's not as well as he pretends, and I'm trying to teach him to mind, but he insists on talking. I told him to stay in there an hour, so we shall have perhaps twenty minutes alone. Let's hurry."

Not quite half an hour later the blue gown reappeared, and stealthily moved over to the window, smoking a cigarette. Gorky had three or four Russian magazines in his hand.

"We'll have to finish this another time," Mme. Budberg told me, "Mr. Gorky won't keep still another minute." And he didn't. He walked over to us, and put his huge hand over our manuscript.

"Listen to this," he says, chuckling, "I'm going to read you something. Tell Clark to give me all his attention."

He reads, with solemn emphasis and an unsuccessful attempt to keep a straight face, what was evidently a poem.

"Tell me what it means?" I ask our interpreter, and she turns to Gorky. He laughs so hard that he brings on a coughing spell. Then he explains that this sample of new Russian poetry is just as clear to me as it is to him.

"Why do they print such stuff!" he groans. "Maybe it's to prove that all writers are equal—that Free Verse is for Free Men—Lord, I don't know!"

That night we discuss politics for the first time.

About Russia Gorky is not too optimistic. "Revolution never helps a bad situation—it usually only makes it worse. People suffer, rebel, fight for what they want or think they want, only to find that they are still as badly off as before: they substitute one set of chains for another.

"In Russia the situation is worse than usual because Russian workmen won't work. They have nothing to look forward to, and they are without ambition. For that matter, the same thing is true all over Europe. In America I think things are different: there the worker doesn't lay off the moment he has enough money to fill his belly with food."

These bits of conversation, which I recorded immediately after my visit as accurately as I could, were punctuated with much hilarity, by the lighting of innumerable cigarettes, by great gestures of Gorky's arms, and, as always, by laughter and jokes.

I see, in going over these notes again, that I had to give up trying to put down everything that was discussed, and I resorted—with some hope of remembering afterward—to the expedient of jotting down single words, or parts of sentences.

It was getting late, and even Mme. Budberg thought it time for the unexhausted and inexhaustible Gorky to go to bed. From the time I started to put on my coat to the moment I left, we discussed Pushkin and his poetry; the preface I got Gorky to write for "my" translation of *The Judge;* the plays of Synge, Benavente and Sem Benelli, whom he considers among the best modern playwrights; the modern European theater; the necessity for making "cultural" movies; the importance of education and books; the ignorance of the Russian peasant; the joy of life; *Boris* at the Dresden Opera; projects for the magazine *Besseda*; two new novels he is working on; and a series of books based on his diaries.

I haven't the least doubt that if Mme. Budberg and I hadn't gone downstairs and prevented Gorky from following us, we would have talked all night.

The following month the Gorky menage went South. On the 18th of June Mme. Budberg wrote: "I have just received your letter and hasten to let you know our address. It is Guntherstal bei Freiburg-in-Breisgau, Hotel Kyburg. It is very comfortable here, but so frightfully rainy and cold! It is most depressing, this climate. Both Mr. Gorky and I are looking forward to see your article—he sends you his kindest regards."

On September 30 I arrived at Guntherstal, a tiny village

two or three miles from Freiburg in the Black Forest. It was early Sunday morning, and I had no idea when my Russian friends would be stirring. The address given me was the Hotel, but that was only the place they got their mail: they lived in a small villa nearby, a pleasant stucco house with a tiny garden.

When I arrived about ten o'clock everyone was up: Gorky was busy talking to a Russian refugee, Mme. Budberg was planning the noonday meal, and young Pyeshkov had just got back from playing tennis at a neighboring club. He and I sat on the porch a while talking. In the early days of the new regime in Russia he had held some government position under Lenin. One of his jobs was visiting the small rural centers, and explaining to the inhabitants the broad outlines of Soviet ideology.

"A discouraging job," he said. "The hardest thing was to establish contact between the peasants and the government. They were afraid of all officials—to them an official meant someone who was going to harm them. Many of these people were incredibly ignorant. In one village they didn't know till eight months later that the World War was over, and their idea of it was that Russia, England and Germany, as allies, were fighting the rest of the world."

Mme. Budberg then joined us. The culinary plans had been rather complicated because Gorky was going to cook the evening meal himself, and insisted on having several exotic and unprocurable articles of food. She went on to say that "Mr. Gorky was very much interested in the formal questions you sent him about your Intellectual Entente idea, and answered them on paper in some detail. He said he preferred doing it that way to taking up time on long abstract discussions when you came here. "When he's cooking he can't be bothered talking world affairs."

Gorky's health has improved since he left Saarow, and he's now at work on a long novel—about a Russian merchant who loses everything when the Revolution comes.

He is pretty tired of the Germans, he says, and their child-ish complaints. He tells me the present economic and political upheaval is fast stripping off the thin veneer of their civiliza-tion, and showing the dumb brute beneath.

Two incidents, I find in my notes, had recently angered him in Freiburg. Three days before, one of his beautiful Per-sian cats had been wantonly shot by a neighbor—the spoiled son of an old-time "noble" general. Young Pyeshkov saw the lad fire the shot. He and the German began to fight, but Mme. Budberg came out just in time to stop them. As she was hurry-ing Pyeshkov back home, along comes Gorky brandishing a heavy cane—swearing he's going to kill the fellow. Mme. Budberg now had her hands full, but she managed to calm Gorky, who swore loud and long. The youth, who was standing by, caught just one word he said—"Idiot." Gorky tried again to assault the culprit, but Pyeshkov and Mme. Budberg man-aged to hold him off and lead him back home.

The other incident was this: "The entire household went in to the city to see a movie. As they entered the darkened the-ater they walked right into the midst of some kind of scuffle. A man had got into a dispute with the cloak-room woman, and the bystanders just looked on and let the fellow beat and kick his victim. Gorky walked right through the crowd, and again Mme. Budberg barely prevented him from punishing the of-fender. 'The German,' Gorky remarked, 'has no manhood.' "

Gorky's caller had now departed and Gorky was relieved. He joined us a moment after he had shut the garden gate.

"That was a man," he announces, "who wanted to know the truth about the report that Chaliapin and I were going to open a palatial house of prostitution on the Riviera."

"What did you tell him?" I ask.

"I said we were." This, to Gorky, was a magnificent joke.

We ask him to sit down but he swears sitting is only for invalids, and *he* is no invalid! He paces back and forth playing with his little black cocker, Kuzka.

"I've been going through my novel, *Mother,* the last few days, wondering if it would make a good movie. I think it would; I'll make a detailed outline of it, and maybe you can help me sell it in America. I could outline other stories, too—the older Russian classics. D'you think that worth doing?"

This is not so much a direct question as an "I wonder" thought expressed in words. He waits for no answer, but goes on, hardly stopping for breath.

He has put on his Sunday best, a neat blue serge suit, somewhat shiny, a soft shirt, and a carelessly arranged necktie.

After discussing the possibility of having *The Judge* translated into Yiddish, and describing the article on Modern Drama he is writing for me, he turns to Mme. Budberg, and insists that she tell me the whole story of Frank Harris's visits. I had got the facts twisted when I last went to Saarow, and more had happened since that day.

It is a long story, but some of it is worth telling. Harris had first turned up when Mme. Budberg was away, and young Pyeshkov did the interpreting. Gorky was called in, and Harris demanded an interview. Not knowing, or pretending not to know who Harris was, Gorky had simply shrugged his shoulders. Harris tried him with French, German, and Russian, and afterward declared he "knew that Gorky understood, but was just trying to insult him." Harris, disgusted, then turned to Pyeshkov, and demanded that he ask Gorky why he had left out of his autobiography practically all references to sex. Gorky just looked at him, said nothing, and went back upstairs.

A few days later Harris had telegraphed from Berlin asking for another appointment. This time Mme. Budberg was present. And again Gorky—who had been told about Harris —remained cool, while Harris delivered a long lecture on sex to Mme. Budberg. At first she had been amused, and then disgusted.

The last time Harris tried to get anything out of Gorky was when he met them in Berlin and took them to lunch at the Fürstenhof.

"No interview that day," smiled Mme. Budberg. "He made love to me, while Mr. Gorky sat staring at us, smoking in silence."

"Let's forget Harris," says Gorky, who is bored having to listen to a conversation of which he understands only the general drift. "Mme. Budberg tells me I knew all about the man the very first time he came to see me. She lies. I'm an ignorant boor!" And he solemnly crosses himself.

The talk veers now to generalities—war and peace and international understandings. "War," he declares, "calls forth very little courage. Most soldiers are afraid—why shouldn't they be? The greatest courage a man can show is to refuse to fight when others are fighting." Mme. Budberg adds a word here: "When I was in prison in Russia (it was Mr. Gorky who got me out at last) the one thing I was most afraid of was showing my fear to others."

"I believe," Gorky goes on, adding to a written passage in his answer to my questionnaire, "that in the long run education, culture, the mind of man—these intangible forces—will do away with war. I have no scepticism or doubt about this, only a strong and (perhaps?) childish faith that it is so."

At the dinner table Gorky has no "manners": he laughs and talks as he eats; crumbles his bread, reaches in front of others. Though he loves to talk, he can be a good listener. He talks straight at you with a half smile, sets his square jaws, and clucks quietly, his small blue eyes always ready to close in laughter.

After lunch we go into the garden, where Gorky, having taken off his coat and put on a gray sweater-vest, applies himself strenuously to weeding the strawberry patch. He's immensely proud of his little garden.

"He's not an expert," Mme. Budberg explains, "but he loves puttering, and it's so good for his health."

I take several snap-shots of him, stooping to examine a vine, bending over, rake in hand. The whole time he smokes cigarettes through his long white holder.

I ask him to pose, and he takes various positions.

"Moujik!" I call him, and he streaks his face with dirt, and bends way over.

"Now be a good Tolstoyan," I say, and he adjusts his tie, looks very serious, and holds the rake delicately between his fingers. "Sorry," he says, "I should be wearing a silk shirt to be in character!"

Preparations for the evening meal had begun early. Gorky quickly changes his gardener's costume for something that resembles a chef's, and for two hours he goes to work in the kitchen, occasionally coming into the living-room to tell us something, or to offer us a sample of his cooking. As appetizers he brings in large slices of bread covered with bits of grated cheese.

There are two or three new faces at the dinner table, Russian friends who have come from Heaven knows where. Everyone is in high spirits, especially when they smell the saucepans that Gorky brings in for our critical approval. As a compliment to his Russian guests he has made special dishes peculiar to the district from which each had originally come.

Though a good deal of the talk is about food, literature and politics are also discussed at great length.

"Which do you think is the better writer?" Gorky asks me, "Chekhov or Andreyev?" He is really not interested in my opinion, he only wants to tell everyone at the table that Chekhov has been overrated, and Andreyev a greater genius than his now famous contemporary.

"Chekhov lacks the seriousness and profundity of Andreyev. But he was no fool. He knew that his plays were basically satirical comedies, and he was annoyed by the Moscow Art Theater people for turning them into sociological documents—even tragedies. The trouble is that Chekhov was practically forced into the theater: his talent was for fiction, not drama."

"But you, Mr. Gorky," I remind him, "ought really to prefer Chekhov's plays to Andreyev's. Andreyev is a tragic writer, and you—from what you have told me—are what we Americans call a Tired Business Man."

"What's that? I thought your business men were never tired?"

I explain my meaning, and he clucks a moment, then answers with all seriousness.

"On the rare occasions when I go to the theater, I make sure beforehand that the play offers some relief to the tragic realities that fill our daily existence."

"That is just what our Tired Business Men tell their high-brow wives when they refuse to go to the theater to see the plays of Ibsen, Tolstoy—and Gorky!"

"Ah, with Gorky it's different!—But I'm not so sure, at that."

It was almost midnight before anyone thought of getting up from table. I was sleepy, and I thought I saw Mme. Budberg look apprehensively at her charge. I had an early train to catch in the morning, and I said so to Gorky. He walked out to the side porch, and into the garden with me. Standing against one of the pillars and looking up at the stars, he murmured softly to himself. Then he called Mme. Budberg.

"Tell this young man," he said, "that we are going to Italy soon, and I don't know when I shall see him again. I'm afraid maybe we have impressed him as a thoroughly trivial and un-Russian lot. So—perhaps it is fitting for me to end on a serious note! Tell him to take this message home with him:

"Nations that have no art, no science, seem to us practically non-existent. For example, we think of the inhabitants of the Dark Continent as belonging to the 'inferior races' because there is no Emerson, no Thoreau, no Sargent, Edison or Carrel among them. It is the artists who actually *create* the souls and indeed the physiognomies of the men of various races. It would be difficult to conceive of Germany without her great artists, or of any nation we recognize as great. It is these men who have created the 'intellectual sympathy' you speak of; it already exists. It is owing to their influence that I, for my part, explain the motives for the generous support given by the American people to the starving peasants of Russia. Without knowledge and sympathy, aroused and disseminated by artists and scientists everywhere and at all times, would America have been ready, as she was, to put herself so whole-heartedly at the service of the Japanese earthquake sufferers?"

"I have not the slightest doubt that political internation-alism will be a *fait accompli* the moment men learn to treat each other in a wise and humane manner. The process has be-gun: science is international, isn't it? And art, too?"

He pauses a moment to light another cigarette.

"Do I sound impressive? I'm trying my best to." This with a boyish smile. "I believe in art, science, education; the novel, poetry, history; the motion picture; I believe in man—and—" He stopped. "Isn't that enough for you? Now I must go back to my guests. The evening is just beginning for them: you see, they are Russians!"

He lays his hand affectionately on my shoulder, turns and making a mock military salute, goes into the house.

JOHN GALSWORTHY

&

HIS WIFE

JOHN GALSWORTHY

T HE Galsworthys had just landed in this country to see the opening of *The Pigeon*, which Winthrop Ames was producing at the Little Theater in New York. This was in 1912, some time before John Galsworthy became front-page news. In our local Chicago paper on page 8 I read a tiny notice informing the few people who might be curious that the English author had arrived in Boston, planned to go at once to New York, and then proceed west to Arizona.

We youngsters at the University of Chicago had a dramatic club, and we were riding high on the wave of what was then, but recently, the New Drama. We were in on a glorious new Renaissance, our own, and its center was Chicago. Some years before, William Butler Yeats had come to supervise what was I think the first performance in this country of *The Land of Heart's Desire*, and a little later Eleanora Duse had addressed our Club membership. Moody had only recently died, and on our faculty we had Herrick, Boynton, Manly, Moulton, and Linn—all of them writers. We were most of us Shaw worshippers, and once we conspired (unsuccessfully) to give a private production of *Mrs. Warren's Profession*. We did manage to do the relatively harmless *You Never Can Tell* and we were the first in the Western Hemisphere, or so we claimed, to perform his *Press Cuttings*.

Our activities were wholly extracurricular, and were permitted almost entirely because three or four of our instructors thought it a good idea to let the youngsters know that the theater was alive. Our most sympathetic sponsors were Percy Holmes Boynton, James Weber (universally known as

(29)

"Teddy") Linn, and the novelist Robert Herrick. The President's secretary, David Allan Robertson, occasionally put in a good word for us, though the President himself never saw one of our plays; I'm not sure that he ever saw any play, for that matter. It was in the winter of 1911–12 that we undertook to produce Galsworthy's unimportant early play, *Joy*. I don't think our production was in any way brilliant, and I know we lost money, but, by golly! we *were* trail-blazers. What did we care if the audience had never heard of Galsworthy nor read a line of anything he wrote, didn't even know how to pronounce his name? So much the better. We were highbrows in a day when that word meant "superior to the common herd."

So when I learned that the author had arrived in our land I didn't even bother to suggest that the University send him an official invitation to speak. I had tried that sort of thing before, and I did it again a few years later, when I found it necessary to explain to the authorities who Arnold Bennett was before they would invite him to tea.

I simply wrote a letter, and I was a little surprised to get an immediate reply:

"I think it is *not impossible* that my wife and I may be in Chicago next week. I could come with great pleasure to your Dramatic Club on the express understanding that I *made no speech*, but just chatted and answered questions to the best of my ability." A second letter came two days later: "We arrive in Chicago, Hotel Auditorium, on Wednesday night, for two or three days, and I suggest Thursday evening, any time that you let me know. I look forward to the occasion now that I know I have not to make a speech."

The members of our little Club were excited, though the notice in the students' paper aroused no stir outside our own circle. The year before Nathaniel Peffer, editor of *The Maroon*, our college paper, had graduated, but by the time he left he had managed to interest a few of his readers in something besides the routine athletic notices without which no undergraduate periodical could sell more than a few dozen copies. It was the handful of exceptional men like Nat, and H. R. Baukhage—he had been president of our Dramatic Club and left college a year previously, after getting his degree—who had insisted on bringing distinguished guests to the campus, and the Galsworthy affair was to some extent their doing, though neither of them had been able to attend the party. I was uneasy, because it would be my job to meet the Galsworthys and do what "entertaining" might be called for. It was up to the girls to arrange the informal dinner at our club room, and I was instructed to turn Mrs. Galsworthy over to them as soon as she arrived on the campus. The trouble was I had undertaken to show the visiting couple around during the day, and our supper wasn't scheduled to start till seven.

At ten in the morning I went downtown to the Auditorium Hotel. Galsworthy had written that he would be waiting for me at the desk. I had imagined him as tall, thin, and of pre-eminently distinguished appearance. There was no one like that anywhere so far as I could see. I picked up a room phone and asked to speak with the newly-arrived visitor. At that moment I felt a gentle pull at my sleeve, and turning around, I recognized the man from his pictures, though I had not connected his thin, wiry, short figure, seen a moment before from a distance, with the celebrity I was expecting. The face I saw was somewhat older than the photographs. He was nearly bald, and the tint of the little fringe of hair that remained was a cross between sandy and yellow, already beginning to turn gray. A "little man" is the first impression that came to me when he held out his hand and spoke his name. Distinguished, yes; intelligent; a finely modelled head—of course. But the small mouth and diminutive eyes, these were not what I had expected. His eyes were weak, and he wore a monocle, gold-rimmed spectacles and a pince-nez, sometimes shifting from one to the other half a dozen times in the space of a quarter of an hour.

(31)

What funny ill-fitting clothes he wore! I believe that 1912 was the period of peg-top trousers and baggy coats in this country, and the unpressed, clinging clothes of this little Englishman seemed even more incongruous to me than they would have seemed at a later time. If I had seen Galsworthy on shipboard crossing the Channel I would have put him down as a vicar from some Midland crossroads village, or at most an instructor in Greek at an out-of-the-way college.

If I was embarrassed and unable to talk about anything but the cold March weather and how windy it was on Michigan Avenue, so was he. He wasn't at all high-hat, as I was afraid he might be. He honestly wanted to show himself as affable as he felt; he, too, was trying to behave in a friendly way and find topics of conversation. So he took a cigarette from his pocket and offered it to me, while he lit his own pipe. We got on famously for a moment, since we didn't have to say a thing. I believe now that he found it as hard to understand my American as I did his English, though later in the day we got on much better. We sat in big easy-chairs for a couple of minutes, and then the tension broke as an attractive black-haired woman came up, and my guest heaved a sigh.

Mrs. Galsworthy at once put us at ease. In a second I realized that she furnished the amenities for his social contacts. With "Ada" at his elbow "Jack" was a different man. She knew how to ask questions, and she allowed her husband to answer when she knew he had to, or could do it at all. I had raided our Dramatic Club treasury and I had enough cash to take my guests to lunch and bring them to the University in a taxi, but before starting out on our tour of inspection Mrs. Galsworthy asked whether the Art Institute was far off: she and her husband wanted to see the Innes Room. We walked up the Avenue against a sharp March wind, Jack's Scotch scarf tucked securely inside the collar of his old Raglan coat. Most of the time at the Institute we spent in the Innes Room, though both my guests were impressed by our new Manets and Grecos.

About luncheon at the hotel restaurant I recall very little, except that I was asked to arrange a visit to Hull House for the next day. I phoned Jane Addams, who of course knew about Galsworthy and invited him to see a performance of *Justice* by the Hull House Players. Dear lady, she seemed to know everyone and everything! She even said she remembered me, but she did not ask me to come with my guests. I recall that in our University circle Miss Addams enjoyed the reputation of being the most remarkable person *she* ever knew. We respected her, but we knew her occasionally amusing idiosyncrasies. The world revolved about Hull House.

We walked along Michigan Avenue for a time after lunch and after a leisurely stroll through the loop, we hopped into a taxi. "No, no," protested both Galsworthys, "you really mustn't use one of these things. They're frightfully expensive, you know." I said that we were off for a ten-mile trip and that our Club had already appropriated the money.

"If you say so, then—but really, this is a great extravagance."

During our long ride, desperately trying to make conversation, I happened to remark, apropos of something I don't recall, that at my home we had two Indian maids.

"You don't say! Mark that, Ada—you mean real American Indians?"

"Two full-blooded Senecas," I went on, "from a New York State reservation."

That was astonishing news to them both. Neither had ever seen an American Indian, and as the taxi neared the University, Mrs. Galsworthy asked whether they might stop off and see our Senecas. "It would be just like a Cooper novel." I instructed the driver to take us down Washington Avenue and stop at our house. My eager guests agreed that we should meet the aborigines in the most natural way, in the kitchen, and without warning. The cab drew up, and I hopped out, going round to the back door. This promised to be fun—introducing Laura White Feather and Flora Red Barn to the Galsworthys. But the back door was locked, my parents were away —and this was Thursday—maids' day out!

The Galsworthys were getting ready to join me when I brought them the tragic news. The last ten minutes of our trip no one uttered a word. I felt at the time—and I still do— that my guests suspected me of having invented a dazzling fable. Real Senecas in Chicago!

The taximeter had mounted to well over five dollars, and I was relieved when my guests told me, on arriving at the entrance to University campus, that they "really preferred walking the rest of the way." Mrs. Galsworthy couldn't help remarking to Jack that we had already "gone over a pound!"

The campus in 1912 was not, of course, the imposing complex of quadrangles it is today, but it was, in its fashion, very very Gothic, in a slightly Americanized way. Most deferentially, as though afraid to hurt my feelings, the short-sighted, blue-eyed member of our party ventured to wish that the buildings had been somewhat less English and more in keeping with the frontier traditions of a new city, but when Mrs. Galsworthy and I pressed him to say *what* style should have been used—something modified from the wigwam, or the blockhouse?—he gently confessed that he couldn't say. If this discussion had taken place ten years later, he would certainly have suggested skyscrapers.

At Cobb Hall I took my charges in to the President's office. The Great Man himself was away, and I was afraid that if he had been there I would have had difficulty in identifying myself, let alone my guests; but his secretary was there, and *he* was a great comfort. "Dave" Robertson had read not only the Galsworthy plays, but at least two of the novels, and told Galsworthy how when the Archbishop of York (at least it was *some* distinguished Anglican dignitary) had come to the University a few months before, the name of Galsworthy was mentioned in conversation, and the churchman, with an attempt at affability, had filled a gap in the talk by remarking with an air of wisdom, "Galsworthy? John Galsworthy! Humm! Doubtless one of your young American writers!"

"The Archbishop of York?" Galsworthy repeated. "Yes, that is precisely what I would have expected of him."

On our way from Cobb to Mandel Hall I was not so nervous as I had been earlier in the day. I was more or less at ease; our conversation for the most part was indirect, I asking "Jack" a question, and "Ada" either answering it or giving Jack the proper cue. Of course, every moment of the time I was so impressed by my self-importance, yet at the same time afraid of making a fool of myself, that I must have seemed pretty stupid, but as I look back I think my guests were just as nervous themselves. Galsworthy was, of course, known here and there as the author of *Strife* and *The Silver Box* and a couple of other plays, but his early novels were familiar to only a few readers. As we walked from hall to hall, passing students and an occasional instructor, I couldn't help feeling a little contemptuous: the University of Chicago was never very strong in the arts, and such appreciation for them as existed was found principally among a very few individuals, like Herrick, Boynton, Linn, and Robertson, and—it goes without saying—among a few of us students in the Dramatic Club. (Strange I never met Burton Rascoe when he was a student there. Harry Hansen, to whom I occasionally said *Hello,* was an upper classman.)

Our guests were turned over in plenty of time to an excited reception committee in the anteroom reserved for us at the Reynolds Club. Mrs. Galsworthy shot one parting glance at me as she was taken over by the girls; it was as though she were signalling me not to worry—she would be with us shortly.

I took Galsworthy to the washroom where Robert Herrick was standing before a mirror combing his thin gray hair. There were a few of us at the University, his students mostly, who were fond of Herrick—so far as any of us could feel that way toward a man who was as well known as he for his standoffish manner. Personally, I felt myself on almost intimate terms with him ever since the day when, in his office, he had offered me a cigarette, and I had smoked it in his awful presence.

So, there in the washroom, standing between the distinguished Robert Herrick and the shy John Galsworthy—both of them in my eyes celebrities of heroic mould—I was even less in command of my social graces than I had been earlier in the day. But I managed somehow to introduce the gods to each other, and to hear the Englishman apologize for not having "dressed" (Herrick wore a tux), and then I wanted to run away! The trouble was that, having introduced the two men, I had to take off my coat, wash my hands and face, and make use of the other facilities the washroom offered—and so had Galsworthy. Surprisingly, the Englishman immediately began telling the American how much he liked Herrick's new novel, and Herrick, whose ablutional and other duties were now completed, stood by unconcerned, doing nothing. He could hardly have turned away from us, particularly since Galsworthy went right on talking. Now, in all probability, the whole episode I am sketching took no more than three minutes, and I'm sure that neither of the men was in any way upset: the drama of embarrassment went on solely in the mind of a very self-conscious kid in his early twenties. As we stepped out into the hallway I wished that I might have been spared the spectacle of Herrick combing his hair, and Galsworthy standing—*not* at the wash-basin—in his shirt sleeves, his worn suspenders flapping down behind him, chatting gravely about the future of the American novel.

Our dinner party was informal. There were twenty of us there, some pretending to like the meager "banquet," and some doubtless never asking whether the food was good or bad. We were served a typical college "dinner." As to that, I suspect that Herrick suffered; at least he told me later that maybe we ought to have broken the campus rule that forbade the serving of liquor to students and instructors when they were seated at the same table. Galsworthy, too, would have enjoyed a Scotch and soda.

Seeing how well Herrick and Galsworthy had got on together in the washroom, I was surprised and dismayed to notice how their conversation petered out when we were all together. The natural reticence of each seemed to react on the other in public, and I was afraid the entire affair was doomed. It was then that the ever-ready Ada came to our rescue. Someone asked her husband a leading question and I saw an expression of relief on his face as he laid down his knife and fork, and began, judicially and hesitatingly, to answer it. In the nick of time (actually Mrs. Galsworthy knew precisely when she would be needed) she prompted him, completed his sentence, and carried us on to the next stage, while Jack again took up his knife and fork. But after the table was cleared and our elders were smoking (how we stared at Mrs. Galsworthy when she lighted a cigarette!), the tension eased to a noticeable extent.

The conversation turned to *Strife*. How did the idea of that play first take root in the writer's mind? This was one of a few questions we had prepared to throw into the conversational breach in case of a lull; as a matter of fact, I had seen Galsworthy's answer to this in an English theatrical paper, and I knew he would have something to say:

"One day I saw two men at the club. They were arguing furiously about no matter what, and neither of them seemed able to do anything but convince himself that he was right. I thought I saw in that fruitless argument a play, and I decided that the usual kind of labor-capital dispute would prove effective in the theater if treated as I intended to treat it. Some persons have said that the play was interesting."

This generalization was the author's contribution, but his wife followed it up, and told us how the scene at the club was merely the starting point; how Jack had been attracted by the central ironic idea that neither disputant had the slightest wish to get at the facts, and that each was intent only on stating his own viewpoint. "You recall," she added, "how the last line of the play sums up and points the irony of the entire work?"

And of course we did recall, because we had been seriously studying the Galsworthy plays that winter.

We were getting on pretty well by now, and I think Teddy Linn, who had come late and been pretty quiet, for him, felt he might safely engage our host in a discussion of non-theatrical matters. Teddy Linn was one of the most popular instructors at the University, a forthright, unaffected, hard-hitting fellow with no frills or nonsense about him. As a student in one of his writing courses I was always afraid of his sharp tongue, yet I was sensible enough to know that some of his acid remarks were made solely for the purpose of getting his students to talk back. He told me many years afterward that one of his great disappointments as a teacher was that no student had ever really stood up and tried to contradict him.

Teddy shot his question at the mild little man sitting opposite him, at that moment pretending to sip what was described on our menu as coffee.

"What ever became of a promising young English writer called John St. John? I read a couple of his books a few years ago and wondered if he'd done anything else."

The small blue eyes looked into Teddy's and lighted up. "I think I can tell you," he said, and Mrs. Galsworthy, with a broad smile finished the sentence: "John St. John is Jack—my husband. He used John St. John as a pen-name when he published his earliest books."

I could never get out of Teddy whether he knew the answer and had tried to help us out, or had really wanted information. Anyway, I was grateful to him.

But most of us were not interested in Galsworthy's novels; it must be remembered that in 1912 Galsworthy was far better known as a playwright. At any rate, we were the *Dramatic* Club, and Galsworthy was with us because of his plays alone.

The next question addressed to him was not planned by our committee. A good-natured scene-shifter who had indeed read most of the Galsworthy plays, for some reason wanted to know:

"Er—Mr. Galsworthy—will you tell us why you haven't any children?" Dead silence. In those long-past days we actually knew the meaning of embarrassment.

"I mean—you know—in the plays?"

Galsworthy cleared his throat, expertly dropped his monocle into his hand (I was afraid it was going into the demitasse) and stammered. We waited, but nothing came—even from Mrs. Galsworthy. So someone else spoke, asking whether the scene at the end of the second act of *The Silver Box* was intended to be symbolical. At the same time conversation had begun at the other end of the table, Mrs. Galsworthy telling the girls about the suffragette riots in London, in one of which a prominent leader had attracted a good deal of publicity by her window-smashing exploits. Her husband, taking that for his cue, in answer to the question about *The Silver Box*, cleared his throat again and spoke up: "You will remember that at the end of the act in question Mrs. Barthwick hears the Jones children sobbing outside her open window. She tells the butler to close the window—she doesn't want to hear. The butler does so, but she can't drown out the voices. It was my purpose, I fancy, not to smash windows but to open them."

This is as near as he came to making a speech, and feeling perhaps that he had gone far enough, he replaced his monocle, sat back in his chair, and stared into his coffee cup.

Robert Herrick, who throughout dinner had actually

smiled once or twice, asked Galsworthy about the report, so often heard, that *Justice* had effected certain changes in English prison conditions. The author modestly replied that he felt sure his play had not been the cause, but that recently a few much-needed reforms had indeed been made. It is true, he added, that Winston Churchill had been deeply moved by seeing a performance of the play, and not long afterward the changes were made. Possibly the play had reminded Churchill of something he already knew. At any rate, Galsworthy had not written *Justice* as a reformer, but as an artist.

At this moment Mrs. Galsworthy entered the discussion again, telling how Jack had spent many months visiting the English prisons.

In 1912 the word pessimism had an ominous sound. A "pessimistic" artist was one who, in our eyes, had something the matter with him: he was foreign, perhaps, or ill, or just plain old.

Now, Galsworthy was by some readers considered something of a pessimist, and Teddy Linn, who had already told us in the classroom that Galsworthy was no pessimist ("and what the hell difference if he was?"), again turned to our host, and asked him if he considered his books pessimistic in tone.

"When people call me pessimistic I hardly know what to answer. I can't see why they should consider my looking at things as they are to be any evidence of pessimism. If my works have any social or moral value at all, it is because they urge tolerance, sympathy for the viewpoint of other people, that they seek to combat human *stiffness*, useless conventions, the abuse of authority temporarily delegated to this man or that. I admit I am distressed to hear that any reader of my books thinks me a pessimist. Really, I'm not."

Someone asked him whether he preferred the writing of novels to that of plays, and he answered:

"If I were required to give up one or the other, I should

give up plays. That may be because the novel was my first love, but I am inclined to believe it is because I like the leisurely technique of prose narrative; I take pleasure in weaving the web of character in a novel or a story; and the effect of a novel, I believe, the effect made on the reader, is more enduring than that made by a play. A play like *Justice*, for example, may strike home at once and possibly bring about some much-needed material reform, but in the long run a novel will sink deeper into the public consciousness. It is natural to me, when I write plays, to adopt what I have called an 'austere technique': I must from some inner necessity reduce everything I have to say to the barest essentials. The playwriting game is interesting and challenging, but I prefer writing narrative."

This, too, was a fairly long "speech," and once again the writer lapsed into silence, as his wife explained to us how she played the piano while her husband wrote. From time to time he dropped his monocle, and nodded gravely in Ada's direction, and when she was through there was a long pause: obviously the time had come to release our weary guests.

As I took Galsworthy to the coat-room, I shot one more question at him—about the symbolism in *The Pigeon*.

"I—I—well, I have something to say about that—but—" he was desperately looking for his wife, so I hinted that I could wait for the answer.

"I can *write*," he said with a smile, "somewhat better than I can talk, and if you'll let me do so, I'll answer your question in a letter, after we reach Arizona. And this is what I'll say—only more clearly," and he proceeded lucidly and quickly to tell me what I wanted to know. If I had not got the letter a few days later, I am pretty sure that my record of what he said would be essentially the same; anyhow, here is the letter:

"About those dates in *The Pigeon*. Christmas Eve because of Ferrand's remark: 'He is come, Monsieur!,' and the general tenor of Wellwyn's acceptance of every kind of outcast. New Year's Day because of Ferrand's remark: ''Appy New Year!' which marks the disappearance of casual charity in favor of institutionalism, of the era of outcasts in favor of the era of reformers. April 1 because of the joke at the end of the Humblemen, which symbolizes the fact, or rather the essence of the play, that, while Wellwyn (representing sympathy and understanding) is being 'plucked' all through the play, he comes out and knows he does, on top at the end, as the only possible helper of the unhelpable. I hope this is sufficiently obscure!"

A bitter wind was blowing in from the Lake when we left Mandel Hall and hopped into our waiting taxi, and the "Little Galsworthys," as we had already begun to call them among ourselves, wrapped themselves securely in all the extra clothing they had brought with them. Neither of them was any too strong, Jack "detested travelling," and Ada was suffering from asthma.

"Is it warm in Arizona?" she asked.

I assured her that it was, only to learn soon after that they had found snow at the Grand Canyon. Even I, who knew no other climate than Chicago's, was stiff when we reached the hotel and my English friends bade me good-night. After paying the taxi man I walked to the nearest corner and took a streetcar back home, relieved that our party was over, and our guests safely returned to their room.

. . . . .

Seven years later the Galsworthys were again in America, this time on a semi-political mission. They had, I think, made an earlier trip here as emissaries bearing British goodwill during the War, and though in 1919 their purpose in coming was different, they made no secret of the fact that they were sent as official representatives of their country.

By this time Galsworthy was a Figure. We had corre-

sponded occasionally since the early visit in Chicago, and I
had just missed seeing him in London in 1914. I wanted my
wife to meet him and his wife, so I sent word to him at the
Chatham in New York, inviting them to lunch. "We shall be
very pleased," he wrote, "to lunch with you and Mrs. Clark at
the Algonquin on Thursday next. May I suggest 1:15, as your
note does not? We are bound for a piano recital afterwards,
and not sure of the hour of its beginning."

The luncheon was, I suppose, a success: the food was
good; we had the right kind of cocktails; I put on a new shirt
(possibly even a stiff collar, I was wearing them then); "Mr.
Galsworthy," not Jack, spoke with calm assurance, and Mrs.
Galsworthy, a graver person than I had remembered her,
no longer found it necessary to prompt her husband. He wore
a beautifully tailored cutaway and a pearl-gray tie, and she
wore—well, I don't recall just what, but it was right, and it
didn't look too "English." She was plumper than she had been
in Chicago, and her husband, whose thin fringe of hair was
now pure white and whose features even more distinguished
than they had seemed in the dim pre-war days, was the picture of dignity.

I forget what we talked about, except for one remark of
Galsworthy's, called forth by my telling him about a promising youngster named O'Neill, and that was that most of our
really good playwrights were "outsiders"—not trained in the
theater, but rather those writers with something to say who refused to learn the conventional stage-tricks.

We must have talked about the war, and music, and Galsworthy's new novels,—but my mind is almost a blank; and I
know that Mrs. Galsworthy and my wife talked music. I am
sure that at least once Galsworthy looked at his watch, and
once Mrs. Galsworthy murmured something about being late
for the recital.

We were, "of course," to meet again; there was so much

to talk about; Mr. Galsworthy would read the O'Neill plays I promised to send him; but they mustn't be late now for the recital.—"It has been a great pleasure seeing you again."

A few days later I wrote to suggest a second meeting, but I was too late:

> Alas! Just off from New York.
> Au revoir
>
> JOHN GALSWORTHY.

The Little Galsworthys I left in Chicago on that March night in 1912 had gone off the next day to Arizona, and never returned.

EDWARD SHELDON

EARLY MEMORIES
Address at the Players' Club
Pipe Night

EDWARD SHELDON

I BEGIN these random memories with an apology to all of you who ever ventured to speak of the Palmy Days with affection or regret, for I, a self-appointed champion of the virtues of our contemporary theater, have time and again ridiculed you as the apostles of reaction. Yet here I am in this sanctuary of reminiscences (where in past years I have listened patiently and more or less respectfully to veterans who had trooped with Forrest before the Civil War), presuming to carry you back to the prehistoric era of 1912.—At this point our Toast-master, Mr. Otis Skinner, may be allowed an indulgent smile.

I too was an actor, and something more besides. Who among you today (even on thirty dollars a week, which I got) could enjoy the privilege of helping the property man, lending a hand to the scene-shifter, playing nursemaid to a live horse, holding the script; running errands for the director, ringing up and down the curtain, and "calling" all players in the cast at every performance? How many of you would be allowed to rehearse a nonmusical play for six weeks, and continue rehearsing it another five after the opening, with *no* increase in salary? It was experience I wanted, and every member of the cast and staff saw that I got it. I received program credit as assistant stage manager, while my superior, after teaching me what to do, spent all his time in the dressing-room. Those were the days! You youngsters with your Equity contracts don't know what trouping is. I have no idea what Equity actors are supposed to do about horses and how far they are permitted to mingle with them professionally, but let me tell you a little about *my* horse. The play was *The High Road,* written by

(47)

Edward Sheldon: it was a Harrison Grey Fiske production and the star was of course Minnie Maddern Fiske. The horse was not under contract, because except for the nine weeks' run at the Hudson Theater in this city we were on the road, and a different horse was engaged in each town. Those of you who know of Mrs. Fiske's interest in dumb animals will understand when I submit the under-statement that her solicitude for them was almost pathological. It was my business six nights a week, and two afternoons, to help the property man and local teamster conduct the horse into the theater, rehearse him, persuade him to observe the strictest niceties of behavior, feed him, thank him and escort him back into the alley after his scene was over—and at the same time see to it that the play went on. The entire operation was invariably carried out under the personal direction of Mrs. Fiske. Now Mrs. Fiske was a humane little lady, and I don't for a moment suggest that she neglected anything that might contribute to the well-being of the human part of her company, but each horse that played with us was treated like a prima donna at the opera. On one occasion, in Detroit, we found that our animal was a trifle too broad of beam to pass through the entrance from the alleyway. Mrs. Fiske, with sugar in her hand, spoke to him persuasively, but the horse would not budge; doubtless, being new to the company, he was a trifle slow to understand her, as Mrs. Fiske was not, as you know, distinguished for the clarity of her diction; so there was nothing for me to do but, taking orders from our star, conduct the animal through the unusally large actors' stage entrance, and down a long corridor to the stage itself. A few days later in Terre Haute another horse, this one thin and rather undernourished, showed signs of nervousness: we stood in cramped quarters, he hitched to a buggy with Fred Perry in it pretending to drive, which nearly scared him to death, and I standing behind, holding on to the bridle for dear life. The poor beast had been ordered to stand close to a property lilac bush, and unseen by me, he began nibbling the leaves. Not knowing what he might uproot I pulled him quickly back, but not before Mrs. Fiske, ready to go onstage for her own first scene, waved frantically at me, a gesture that meant, "Touch but one hair of that——horse!" When her scene was over and the beast safely back among the dressing-rooms, our leading lady commanded me to give him an extra portion of oats.

Those Good Old Days—not perhaps the Palmiest, but they were good, after a fashion. There was a broad graciousness, too, and a kind of pleasant formality that bespoke tradition. Actors bowed to each other at rehearsals, and one heard one's self called Mister, though on special occasions (say, when Mr. Belasco or Mr. Charles Frohman was in the house) one of the older players permitted himself to address me as "My dear chap." The heart warmed at such friendly condescension. "Sweetheart" and "Darling" in those faded bygone days were terms used exclusively by persons of opposite sexes on occasions of the utmost intimacy.

These preliminary trivialities, however colorful they may seem to me after so many years, are only incidental to the big thing that filled my existence during that exciting season of 1912–1913. The big thing was Ned Sheldon. Not that I ever dreamed of calling him, or even speaking of him, as other than Mr. Sheldon, young as he was. For it was he who called the horse into being and provided my protean role for me, who recklessly strewed his script with buggies and lilacs, full moons and cowbells, rattling dishes, governors' offices and drawing rooms, fancy rural exteriors, Giorgione paintings and grand pianos, whose notions of grandiose theatrical background would frighten off any but a musical show manager of today. If this young playwright wanted silver ashtrays he got them; if Arthur Byron or Charles Waldron wanted to smoke real Melachrinos in their long scene in Act Two, they got them; Mr. Fiske gave the order and the ubiquitous and accommodating Alice Kauser saw to its execution. Whether all

(49)

plays were mounted so lavishly in 1912 I don't know, but to me it was a matter of course. I am sure that no one in my presence (and I think I was everywhere at the time) ever asked Mr. Sheldon to reduce his five sets to one, or to cut the part of the horse.

Edward Sheldon was the first of the playwriting gods I ever met—I mean American gods. Foreigners didn't count: there had always been a European drama, but I was determined, single-handed if necessary, to see to it that we should have an important native drama of our own. I had been fired by the eloquence of Percy MacKaye, that St. John in the Wilderness, and I had read all about the annual Messiahs who were blazing trails with plays like *The Easiest Way* and *The Great Divide*. I had followed the career of the Boy Wonder from Harvard, thrilled with the daring realism of *Salvation Nell* in 1908, shaken to the depths by the tragic horror of *The Nigger*, and moved and delighted by *The Boss*. The Fiskes had engaged me in August of 1912, and the night I left home I spent without sleep on the Pullman, thinking not so much of Mrs. Fiske, whom I had already met, but of the author. Would he be there? Was there any chance of my meeting him, actually speaking with him and perhaps having him exchange words with me? Writers were strange creatures, I knew.

It was one of those pleasant August afternoons in Manhattan when the thermometer had dropped to about 99, that I found my way to the Lyceum Theater. I went up to Dan Frohman's office under the roof, where I met Mr. Fiske and signed my contract. I was now a professional actor, and stage manager as well (the "assistant" part I uttered under my breath), and the first rehearsal, in the room next to Frohman's office, began. Mr. Fiske, precise, businesslike, worried-looking, sat at a table, twirling his little blonde moustache: Mrs. Fiske, wearing glasses, next to him, looking more like one's aunt from the country than America's best-known actress. Standing next to her and looking twice her height was a low-voiced young man, with the blackest hair and the reddest cheeks and lips. Mr. Fiske summoned me to his table and handed me the bulkiest script I ever saw till *Strange Interlude* came along. My first job, he explained, would be to hold on to the script for dear life, and enter into it every change that might be made by himself, by "Minnie," or Mr. Sheldon. "This is Mr. Sheldon." Just a nod in the direction of the young giant, who nodded back at me, shook hands, and smiled. It was a shy smile, and somehow it didn't seem to belong to the distinguished writer I had pictured to myself. I was a bundle of youthful suppressions and inhibitions, and at the time I was afraid he despised me: after all, I was a critic, even though I had not yet published a word, and critics in the eyes of so-called creative writers are of no consequence.

But that evening, dining alone at Browne's Chop House, surrounded by photographs of Coghlan in *The Royal Box* and Forrest as Virginius and Garrick as Hamlet, I reflected that the theater was a grand place to work in, that Mrs. Fiske was friendly and helpful, and that having met, and won a smile from, Mr. Sheldon I was well launched on my career. I think even that the benevolent Edwin Booth, whose picture faced me at the far end of the corner where I sat, wished me well; and perhaps, some day, Mr. Sheldon would notice me, really notice me.

Then the grind began: morning till night we rehearsed, and Sunday, and holidays, eight, ten, twelve hours a day. Over the week-end before we opened in Montreal we were in His Majesty's Theater for twenty-two hours. You would have thought, from the infinite care lavished on that production, that we were all disciples of Stanislavsky on the first lap of a two-year rehearsal. Mr. Sheldon was always there, looking taller than ever, a thick block of note-paper in hand, eternally whispering, in that velvety voice of his, bending his head way down over a table to discuss script changes with Mr. or Mrs. Fiske. At the end of a weary day, after the company had been dismissed, I would often be summoned to Mrs. Fiske's hotel, where she wanted to rehearse a scene with me—"just a ten-minute run-through"—that stretched out for two hours. Occasionally the author was there, and I would amend my script at his direction.

He came with us to Montreal, and when we in the cast (all but Mrs. Fiske, who never tired) were dropping from exhaustion the author, never raising his voice, would look as though he had just stepped out of a cold bath after a ten-hour sleep. He went down the street and returned with sandwiches and coffee for everyone. If Mr. Fiske showed signs of nervousness or irritation, not so Mr. Sheldon: in a way he held us all together, and always without argument or criticism. The play got mixed notices in Montreal, but you would never know from him that anything was wrong: he encouraged us by his mere presence; we learned, from the stage, to play to his great round eyes that hung suspended out of nowhere in the back of the house. How he did it I don't know, but he could smooth out "situations" that sometimes complicated things when the rest of us were weary and irritated. Once during the last days before we opened Mr. Sheldon, with rather more of a twinkle in his eye than usual, told me that Mrs. Fiske wanted me to listen to her long speech in the last act. "Go way up in the balcony, my dear boy," she called out from the stage, "and listen to this. Mr. Sheldon tells me he can't understand what I say. Mind you, I want you to stop me the first time you miss a word." The point here will be missed by anyone who doesn't know that Mrs. Fiske sometimes spoke what might just as well have been Russian for all the audience could understand of it. I took my place in the balcony and watched the back of Mr. Sheldon's head down in the sixth row. He was laughing quietly to himself. Mrs. Fiske began, and I shook with nervousness. "Can you hear?" she interrupted herself. I could—and besides, I knew the lines. Then she began to speed up, and I stopped her. "What is it?" she asked. "Speak up, my dear boy." "I can't understand you, Mrs. Fiske," I ventured, and she stopped. "You can't? You're not paying proper attention! Thank you, thank you. You may come down now. And never, never, on your word of honor, hesitate to tell me when I become inarticulate." Of course she went on just as she had always done, but I never stopped her again. When I came downstairs Mr. Sheldon grinned as he greeted me: "I've been up in the balcony, too." Of course he did not say these words; he said nothing, but I knew. The incident meant little to him, but to me it was a sign that I had been noticed. I was noticed again not long afterward. I was playing the not very important part of the governor's secretary and Mr. Fiske told me I would have to smoke a cigar: *all* governors' secretaries smoked cigars. I said I'd try, but cigars made me sick. "It is your business as an actor," he explained, "to do as you're told: the manuscript calls for a secretary who smokes cigars." I tried it just once. The author was standing, as usual, way in the back of the house, and he had heard everything. After the rehearsal he beckoned to me and pointed to the manuscript he held in his hand. He had crossed out the stage direction. Next time I didn't smoke, and Mr. Fiske never opened his mouth about it again.

Well, the experience I wanted I got: I learned the difference between a grand drapery and a wood-wing; I had seen a manuscript develop from two hundred pages of paper into a successful drama; I understood that it was bad luck to whistle onstage; I had watched rehearsals until I was dead to the world; I had accomplished the astounding feat of treating horses to the entire satisfaction of the president of the Humane Society; and I had met and actually associated with one of the great white hopes of our native drama. Then in the spring of 1913 I quit.

There remained in my memory the figure of a friendly and gracious young man, whose career had so far demonstrated that he was no flash in the pan. This silent youth gave out few if any interviews; he made no claims as the bearer of any great message to the world; he was, I knew, a humble fellow who was trying to carry over into the theater some of his convictions about modern American life, and he used the stage as an instrument to create those effects that have always been known as "of the theater." Even before the advent of O'Neill he was aware that no matter what a writer has to say or how subtly he may want to say it, the theater's power depends on the writer's ability to use broad and striking effects; in other words, the theater is in many ways a relatively crude medium in which, once in a generation if we are lucky, a great writer speaks through it most effectively by working with, rather than against or in spite of it. Edward Sheldon worked *with* his theater.

The years passed, and other promising white hopes came and went, and once in a blue moon one of them made good; and some of us, eager to speed the day of fulfillment, over praised the new messiah, and forgot the forerunners of an earlier day. And it seemed that Sheldon, whose most conspicuous original work belonged to the years before the First World War, was destined to become only a memory, kept fresh by an occasional revival of *Romance;* but that was not to be, for this young man with a promise, this one-time demi-god of the American theater of his day was born again in a new and strange manner, and managed to deliver to us something of what he had promised in his early youth. This phenomenon, this reaching out and beyond the normal term of his career as a playwright—this extension of his influence—was actually only a continuation of what he began so many years ago. When, after being reduced to complete physical impotence by a terrible malady, he stopped writing plays of his own exclusive authorship, he collaborated, usually with younger dramatists, and brought to bear on such men as Sidney Howard the magnetism of his own personality and the benefits of his mature advice. Important as his early plays were, and much as our contemporaries of today owe to their influence, it is the man whose sympathy and enthusiasm and advice reaches out in all directions, whose mind is constantly alert to catch the overtones of writers and actors many of whom carry to him their problems and their hopes—it is this man, I say, who is in a way our ideal audience, our sounding-board, the man of whom we may always be sure that he is listening. This I had known for years, for it is common knowledge, but once, a year ago, I said a few words over the air and they had touched something in Sheldon's consciousness. He was the first who told me he liked what I said, and the friendly wire he sent only a few hours afterward showed me that he had taken notice of me, for the third time in my life. That pat on the shoulder is the kind of thing that is always happening when he is around. It brought back to me the picture of the tall young man with the quizzical and friendly smile in the dark corridors of the Lyceum Theatre.

GEORGE MOORE
AT HOME IN PARIS

GEORGE MOORE

I AM trying to make a picture of this man as I saw him during several months in Paris in 1922, complete only so far
as my personal perspective can reach, and based almost entirely on a little journal I kept at the time. What follows is, except for connecting paragraphs and an occasional explanatory
comment, a series of jottings made on the spot and at the time,
set down because it amused and interested me to try to record
as accurately as I could just what George Moore looked like,
what he said, and how he said it.

As I write these lines, many years after I spoke with him
for the last time, I am not at all sure whether they will ever be
published as they are now written; and this gives me a feeling
of security, relieves me of the necessity of arranging the material in conventional orderly fashion, dressing it up for public inspection, or cutting out what some might think tactless or
superfluous; for I have a notion about the art, and science, of
biography, an aim which, though impossible to realize, is worth
trying to achieve. It is simply that the more one tells about any
human being, regardless of its actual or imagined relevance,
the nearer one is likely to come to painting an accurate picture.
I do not mean that every sentence uttered by the sitter is
necessarily of equal importance, that every gesture observed
and described illuminates some fundamental characteristic,
or that the observer can by converting himself into a recording
machine, create a perfect likeness or a work of art; yet I think
that by making and setting down a series of faithful and more or
less dispassionate observations one may come somewhat closer
to one's subject than is possible if one were to set out to prove

anything about him, to interpret or explain or definitely "place" him against a background.

At any rate I put down in my note-book everything I could remember about this extraordinary man, who would be worth describing even though he had never written a line of literature. This attempt at a portrait of George Moore, himself an artist in literary portraiture, would be absurd if I had tried to do anything but record what I saw of him and heard him say: I leave to others the difficult task of interpretation, eulogy, and criticism.

During the winter of 1922 my wife and I—she is here referred to as Cecile—lived in a small room in Paris on the top story of the old Hôtel de Ranes, at 21 Rue Visconti. Downstairs in the courtyard lived a joyous and delightful American girl, Catherine Hopkins, who enters my story here and there, a fashion artist who died a few years after the events described; and on the second floor, our old friends Richard and Alice-Lee Myers, also characters in my little narrative.

It was in 1914 that I had first seen Moore. I was in London and, with no better motive than curiosity, I had gone to Ebury Street for an hour's chat. From that time until late in 1921 I had carried on a sporadic correspondence with him, and just after Christmas my wife and I left home and settled in Paris. It was in February that I wrote Moore in London saying that I hoped to see him there later in the year. A few days afterward a uniformed footman from the Hotel Brighton appeared at our door and delivered this letter:

> Dear Mr. Clark: I received your letter, forwarded from London this morning, and am writing to ask you if you are free this evening and if so will you call here at 7:30 and we will dine together.
>
> *Sincerely yours*
> GEORGE MOORE

I wrote a short reply, saying that I would gladly come at the hour named, gave it to the obsequious footman, and began worrying about what I ought to wear. Cecile was undecided

("He may be a crotchety old gentleman, you know!"), and I, on general principles of course was against formal dress, but Dick Myers was called in and he urged that there might be other guests. So I got out my tuxedo, and that was that.

Moore had been sitting at a desk in the writing room of the Brighton and when word of my arrival reached him he made a somewhat dramatic entrance—with just the touch of a flourish. He was dressed in a blue serge suit, with a soft gray shirt and loose collar. The most noticeable thing about him was his pure white silky hair and flowing cream-colored moustache. He looked younger than he did when I had seen him in London seven years before. Dreamy light blue eyes; drooping shoulders; long arms; soft hands with tapering fingers. He stooped a little. As others have often remarked, he is hard to describe. In repose, his face reminds me of the German Kaiser's: mouth stern, eyes set and cold. No, that's hardly right, either. Maybe I can get it later, adding bit by bit. I'll see.

With few conversational preliminaries we walk out into the street. So I dressed, did I? Useless. Now why did I do that? *He* wouldn't have bothered, but no matter, let it pass. We walk on, a long way, through narrow by-streets to the Boulevards, all the way to the Boulevard Montmartre, and turn a little way up the Rue d'Hauteville. What restaurant? I forget the name, but I think a famous old place, a familiar haunt of Moore's. Moore was a little nervous as he came in; he had had a bad time crossing streets, dodging taxis and cursing at them under his breath. I had tried to pilot him through crowds and between crazy buses, but that wasn't easy: he clung tight to his closed umbrella, held under one arm, and gesticulated as he talked with the other. But in the restaurant he calmed down in a moment and studied the menu as though he were reading proofs. He ordered dinner in the old ceremonious manner, asking and taking advice from the waiter and the *patron*. Turning to me, "You like this soup?" he asked, but didn't wait for my answer. Summarily he dismissed the waiter with, "Garçon, deux soupes!"—Now what in the name of heaven were these *Coquilles St. Jacques*? The waiter tried to explain but failed to satisfy Moore, who ventured his little joke. "Are they Saint-Jacques *Rousseau*?" The *patron* now enters the scene, and makes his explanation, but Moore is irritated. Let it pass, let it pass.

It was a rather long evening, and I was occasionally ill at ease when the conversation lagged, but later I forgot my embarrassment as Moore gathered momentum. We talked for more than three hours, and what about? A good deal of what he said, and the words he used in saying it, can be read in his books, for Moore certainly repeats himself, but there was a good deal new that I remembered later. We rambled far and wide, and there was no unity to the whole thing, for Moore brings a subject to an abrupt close the second it no longer interests him. That is the reason why parts of my record are so disjointed.

He had just read Donnay's celebrated play, *Amants*, an old favorite of mine that I had translated several years before. He thought it distinguished as writing, but objected to it because it depended upon what seemed to him a more or less remote, almost imaginary, world of social standards and behavior. I ventured to suggest that both the writing and the sentiment in *Amants* reminded me of Moore himself in his early efforts as a novelist.

"What's that? Oh—." He seemed not to have heard what I said, and his eyes went dull. Then, apparently, Donnay's play reminded him of his own comedy, *The Coming of Gabrielle*. Nigel Playfair, he said, who had recently thought of producing the play in London, had no proper notion as to how it ought to be acted. So Moore said. Playfair insisted, for example, on cutting out important speeches. Moore claimed he had attended only one rehearsal, but that was enough for him. " 'Good God, man!' " he quoted himself as saying to the producer, 'what if I asked you to dinner and offered you a lemon, one solitary lemon! You wouldn't like it, would you, but you would eat it for politeness' sake! Suppose then I gave you a second lemon, and another, and then another?' My God, the man has no sense of variety in his directing. I was on my sixth lemon and was heartily tired of it. Besides, that last lemon was green! I put a stop to our agreement and everything was over between us. But after I forced Playfair to drop the play I had many offers, especially from actresses, but I suppose—tell me, do you think the play would interest America?"

Before I could answer he went on to say that he would like to make a dramatization of *The Brook Kerith*. "If a good manager offered me proper encouragement I'd write it. But I am not sure, I do not know; that would mean a year's hard work for me."

Speaking of *The Brook Kerith,* he was reminded of what St. John Ervine wrote of it, that it had been conceived from three different viewpoints. "What unspeakable nonsense! What does he know of writing? Ervine! The man is quite devoid of critical judgment or talent!"

Plays. His mind runs to plays, mostly his own. We fell to talking about the dramatized version of *Esther Waters,* which I had recently re-read. I said I thought he ought to revise it, and try to sell it to an American producer.

"Oh, no, I'm weary of that play. I shan't bother with it again, but why don't you do it?"

"I'm not a playwright."

"How do you know you're not a playwright? You should be ashamed to say that. Try your hand at this new *Esther Waters* play. Perhaps we could do the work together. Your interest would stimulate my own. What do you say?"

I tried to pass this off as a joke, but Moore evidently meant what he said.

"If you care to undertake the work, read the play again, think it over, and when I come back to Paris in a few weeks you can tell me what you are prepared to do."

I was still sceptical, though I did make up my mind to

re-read the play, but a moment later plays were forgotten, Moore turning his thoughts toward the projected Carra Edition of his works which was soon to be brought out in America. He had just seen Horace Liveright in London, and Horace had proved a disappointment. "A queer specimen, indeed, but since no other publisher cares to bring out a new edition of my writings in your country I am satisfied to let Liveright go ahead. The fellow prefers books that he calls a little 'off color', and he is always plaguing me to write such things. He wants me to reprint *Flowers of Passion* and *Pagan Poems* and *Mike Fletcher*; he thinks these would advertise the Carra set, and enable him to boast to the public that he's giving them a hundred-pound book for six dollars." Moore pretended to be disgusted; the Carra Edition, he says, is to include only the work by which he wants to be remembered. *Evelyn Innes* and *Sister Teresa*, as well as the volumes of verse and *Mike Fletcher*, are under no circumstances to be resuscitated.

"No, no, I will not give in to Liveright. To allow that early trash to go into the new edition would be what I call the *Concessions of a Young Man*." He bared his large teeth and smiled complacently.

It was a tiny smile, and he waited to see how I reacted to his execrable pun. I smiled back, uncertain what was expected of me. Then he began thinking aloud.

Celibates he has no use for. "That book is full of unspeakable things." *In Single Strictness* will probably be the title of the re-written volume that is to take its place. New stories, he says, all of them, not rewritten versions of the old ones. *Spring Days* he likes; he has always liked it, but *Mike Fletcher* fills him with horror. "Don't speak of that awful book!" He hopes no one will ever find a copy of it.

Avowals does not satisfy him; there is much there to be re-written. *Literature at Nurse?* An early trifle, the essence of which he has incorporated into the *Address to the Jury* in *Avowals*.

Hail and Farewell shall stand as it is. "I will never read that book again. I have nothing more to add to it. It is a good work, I think."

The Brook Kerith has just been issued in a revised edition, but most of the rewriting was limited to minor verbal matters. "I did shocking things in that book, and there remain even now many more changes to be made. Yeats, whose business it is to befog everything, told me when I was writing it that he hoped I would use the 'You' form and not the 'Thee' and 'Thou.' I wrote the first chapter that way and it was all, all wrong. What a hell of a time I had putting back the 'Thees' and 'Thous'! But there is one passage in the book (it may be in the two-volume Tauchnitz edition) where the 'You' form remains. I shall let that stand. I used the same forms in *Héloïse and Abélard,* for I knew how to handle them when I wrote that book. I enjoy using the archaic forms. They are right—right."

When Moore began eating he had shown some interest in food, but now that he was talking about his books he looked up wonderingly and a little irritated every time the waiter uncovered a dish or asked a routine question. He was well launched in a discussion of *Impressions and Opinions,* and for ten minutes he left his food untouched. So did I.

"I cannot understand how I came to write such horrible stuff as I did in some of those essays. Most of the papers are exceedingly poor. Yet I shall keep the *Degas,* and *Mummer Worship;* perhaps one or two others; I shall re-write them and bring together material for another book that will go into the collected edition. There are some good things in the old volume, too; I don't understand how I was able to write such first-rate papers as the two I just mentioned. *Mummer Worship* is particularly good. I still like it."

"You ask me about *A Mummer's Wife.* Vilely written; I did that novel before I had learned the art of writing; I was an apprentice. But you will have noticed how much better the revised version is. People tell me not to revise my old books; but am I to allow them to stand as they are? Dear, no!"

I ventured to say that I was amazed to see how dispassionately Moore could look upon his own work, and that he and Jules Lemaître seemed endowed to an extraordinary degree with the ability to regard every book, their own or others', as though they had never before heard it mentioned. "How do you account for that?"

The blue eyes focussed on me, seriously, almost accusingly. "About the other man you speak of, I don't know, but for myself, I'd say it was because I have never been educated. I educated myself; I am still learning. I suppose that's the answer."

He was just as bitterly critical of his own work as he was of that of his contemporaries, except that he does claim that some of his own books are good. "I see clearly," he went on, "just what I have done, the good and the bad. I have perspective, too. I happened to come upon the literary scene at the right moment, being present at the beginning of an important artistic and literary rebirth. I came to France, as I have often said in my books, and I became a Frenchman. I think I would actually have become a French writer if I had not lost my money and been forced to return to England, in order to support myself. It was in England that I forced myself to learn the English language. Before that I had become saturated with French art and literature. I wrote the first 'serious' novels in the English language! I invented adultery, which didn't exist in English fiction until I began writing. Now, I simply happened—that's all. If I had been born at another time and in another land I might, indeed—For God's sake (this to the waiter), now what is that? Don't interrupt us!"

"Where was I when the fellow came?—Oh, yes. I might indeed have become a writer, but what I wrote would have been without point or meaning."

The waiter had interrupted the flow of Moore's thoughts, and he ate in silence until I attracted his attention.

"No, I don't think I shall ever lecture in America. I have many good American friends, but I am afraid I should not like your country. You Americans all tell me so.—What? You don't agree? Doubtless you are prejudiced. So be it. But I did sign a contract to deliver a series of lectures; or rather, three lectures, which I planned to read from a manuscript; but nothing came of that plan. I got nervous for fear I had not enough to say; no particular message to deliver. And, you know, I'm a very poor sailor. Then, too, I feared the receptions and meetings, all the entertainment; and, Oh good God! Those dreadful long train trips. No, I could not have endured that. And the contract I was supposed to sign! Incredible! Among other things, I had to promise that I would travel alone. I dare say the agent was afraid I would take some woman with me! I wrote him asking for an explanation of that paragraph, and the agent answered, apologetically, that it was a mere formality. He must have been thinking of the Gorky scandal."

I told Moore of the Tagore and Maeterlinck tours, and since he had himself raised the point, I added that a few foreign celebrities had made a lot of money lecturing. "How much would I make?", he asked. He was more amused by this idea than seriously concerned. I don't think he is much interested in the mere making of money. I explained that he could not expect to earn as much as the headliners whose books sold by the hundred thousand, because the public interested in his work was comparatively small.

"I see, I see, so I suppose that I shall never go to America. And there is little reason why I should. I am not curious about your manners and customs and modes of speech, because in spite of the fact that so many people tell me of the striking differences between Americans and Englishmen, especially in the matter of speech, I can see none at all. The American speech I have heard seems to me more genuine and unaffected than our so-called English." But he recalled with great amusement one experience with Americans that he recounted in some detail:

"Not long ago I was travelling from Paris to Nantes, where I had gone to investigate some matter having to do with the background of *Héloïse and Abélard,* and I met two American sailors—they were in the Navy. From your Middle West —Iowa, I think. I met them again soon after, at a Duval restaurant. Seeing that they could speak no French, I went to their table and ordered their food for them. I sat down and we had some desultory conversation, and they told me they were going to England the next day. 'So am I,' I said. 'To learn English?', they asked. I couldn't understand what they meant by that, until they explained that they had never heard an educated Englishman speak English. I didn't tell them I was Irish: that would have confused them: they thought I was French."

The talk now drifted to Paris, as was natural, and I asked how the Paris of today affected him. The physical Paris, the streets and houses, seemed to make little impression on him; his thoughts went back to the city of his youth. "In France," he mused, "art is dead. The last real painters were the Impressionists. Of course, the Paris of one's early days is an impossible imaginary Paris, but it is by all odds the best—for me. No new art has come to us since the days of Manet and his contemporaries." And that settled the matter.

I recall very little else that was said during our long dinner, but I remember the feel of the drizzle as we walked quickly along the Boulevards. We paused a moment by the entrance to the Passage des Panoramas, and Moore pointed with his umbrella down the arcade toward the room on the second floor where he had lived for many months during the seventies. We were about to go into the Passage when the rain began to beat down upon us, and Moore raised his umbrella. "Never mind now," he said, turned on his heel and went out again. On leaving the restaurant he had seemed to me very tired, but somehow our moment's pause recalled memories, and he strolled off toward the Boulevard and reminisced at random as we made our way back to the Hotel, dodging taxis

and buses. Moore poured himself out on the subjects of popular education, art, literature, and the theater. Why, he wondered (we were making a difficult crossing in front of the
Madeleine), should we dread the possible extinction of all artistic production as an unmitigated evil? Perhaps the human
race is destined to produce no more art at all? But what of it?
Have we not enough to delight us for a long time to come?
Suppose the age we now live in fails to inspire a new and vig-
orous art? That might be a very good thing. Let us not bewail
the possibility. "Sometimes I feel that education, as we are
dispensing it, will result in the destruction of art. In some ways
education is a dangerous, a damnable thing."

Why Verlaine should have come into his mind as we
hurried along by the Café Royale, I don't know, but Verlaine
was the subject at that moment. "Verlaine was an extraordinary conversationalist; he had an acute sense of sound, and
liked hearing himself talk. He loved to roll out his sentences,
slowly, with marked emphasis." Moore quoted, verbatim he
claims, a little anecdote as Verlaine told it to him, but I am
afraid I both misunderstood the point (which he declared was
obscene) and failed to recall the last part of it. Anyway, here
is what Verlaine is reported to have said: "J'avais une demi-
heure d'attente à une petite gare. Je traversai le pont et je
vis un grand homme avec une belle barbe noire. Il—" what
he said or did I just don't know. Moore accompanied and punctuated this with sweeping gestures and a voice like a cathedral
organ.

Silence now for a few moments, then the subject of Arnold Bennett seemed worth discussing, and Moore tried it out.
Moore had been fairly familiar with Bennett's work for several
years before the two had met. They had corresponded often,
and Moore was flattered when Bennett acknowledged indebt-
edness, in a literary way, to his "spiritual" father. "Bennett
called me that, and I appreciated his saying so in public. I
have known many fathers in the flesh to be gratefully acknowl-

edged by their sons, but in the matter of art it is usually a very different matter. So we met at last, Bennett and I: he's a charming fellow; I am immensely fond of him and I imagine he has a liking for me. An astonishing man—an amazing mind. Do you know how he works? Well, he sits down at his writing table when he is ready to start a new book, calls the maid, has her fetch him his paper (the finest quality antique), his box of water-colors and a glass of water. He then paints an elaborately decorated title page, like the illuminated manuscript of some 12th century monk, and covers it with huge lilies and dimpled cupids. It is all very nicely and neatly done—but in rather doubtful taste. He then fills in the title with ornamental lettering, using the blackest of black ink. Then he starts writing, and goes straight ahead without pause or the use of notes, and never alters a word or a comma. Not a single word. When he showed me the huge manuscript of *The Old Wives' Tale* I asked if he had written that in the same way, and he pointed out several pages. The first and only draft! I could not believe my eyes. Not an erasure. I declare I couldn't have written that opening description of the Midlands without working it over a dozen times. I would most certainly have got things all mixed up; the proportions would not have come right until after I had written or dictated many versions and revised them with the greatest care and trouble. Most writers would have had to do the same thing, but not Bennett: he tells me he never even looks at a manuscript after he finishes the first and only draft. Yes, an interesting fellow; when you and Mrs. Clark come to London you must meet him and learn to know him. I shall ask Bennett to dinner, and I shall order—."

I never found out what he planned to order, because the talk suddenly veered to Anatole France. "That man is always sucking a lollypop. That's all his writing amounts to!" He was especially disdainful of *Thais*. At first I didn't know what book he was speaking of because he (apparently) went out of his way to mispronounce the name. "Tinsel, that book is, cheap tinsel." I was naive enough to take issue with this judgment, but Moore looked at me compassionately, and his eyes went dull as they do when a subject no longer interests him. He said no more at this time about Anatole France.

If he was severe on the Frenchman he was savage toward Thomas Hardy. "Hardy doesn't write English at all. Servant-girl literature," he muttered as he shook the rain from his umbrella, folded it, and strode into the lobby of the Brighton. "Melodrama, cheap melodrama."

I faced a long walk home, and I was ready to leave, so I suggested that since it was past midnight Moore might want to go to bed.

"Bed? Why suggest that? Are you bored? Let us sit here in the writing-room and talk about Pater. Do you smoke cigars? No matter. Sit down. Are you familiar with Vernon Lee's work?—Some of it?—Oh, you admire her writing! Never mind. Not long ago she came to see me, I don't remember why. We had not met for thirty years. Maybe it was to tell me that she liked *The Brook Kerith*—yes, that was it—mm—a very good book! The name of Pater was mentioned by her or by me, I forget, and I told her, 'The poorest page of Pater is better than the best I ever wrote.' Vernon Lee reflected for a moment on that and answered with a smile, 'Yes, I think that may well be so, it is almost true.' I liked her frankness, for she spoke the truth."

"I am certain," I put in, "that your writing is more supple and colorful than Pater's, more flexible, more musical. In larger doses Pater wearies me a little. But perhaps I am too immature to appreciate Pater fully."

"You are, my young friend, you are. I sometimes think I am myself only beginning to appreciate him. Pater wrote better than I write, better than I shall ever write, because he had a finer mind than I have. You can't write beyond your mind. I admit that there is what may seem to some readers a kind of monotony in Pater's writing, and he has no humor, but it's so easy to be facetious (that's one thing that's wrong with Bennett); I have great difficulty keeping smart aphorisms and humorous passages out of my own work. Pater knew better than that. He knew what was right and what was futile and frivolous."

Moore wondered what effect dictation would ultimately have on literature, and remarked that he found it easy to dictate, especially his first drafts. He merely gets his ideas down in this way, in order that he may know what to discard and what to use. As a rule he cannot dictate at first even a paragraph that will satisfy him. It must be gone over and over again to make it right—ready for publication. "Can you imagine," he asked, "dictating all the descriptions in a novel, and all the dialogue, everything in its proper order, with due regard for balance, turning out so much a day, day in and day out, shutting off the tap at four o'clock and starting in again next morning? Oh, out of the question! I couldn't do that. I have to write and rewrite, scratch out, revise, dictate, re-dictate. What I have set down upon paper at first is hardly more than a skeleton of what will remain as the finished product. Many pages of what I publish have been pulled to pieces and revised twenty times, at the very least."

Returning now to Pater he repeated, as though to himself, "You can't write beyond your own mind. Pater knew that, and he had a great mind."—The subject of Pater was then definitely closed, and I again suggested that it was high time for me to go home. A long pause; an accusing glance from the blue eyes; another question to be asked: "Tell me, you have come so recently from America, how do you account for this American reform mania? Good God, you are always trying to make your people behave. It's absurd, isn't it?" Prohibition and literary censorship in particular roused his anger.

"It's all the fault of that damned Mayflower. What is the meaning of it all? *You* think it's absurd, don't you? I have met many of your fellow-countrymen and had letters from them.

They are all reformers, aren't they—as though reform were a business or profession. Perhaps it is? But you are English over there, aren't you? Traditionally, at least. Yes, it is the Anglo-Saxons who are the chief offenders. Your Germans and Russians and Jews and Poles are not reformers, are they? Yes, yes, in England it began with Jeremy Collier and his attacks on Congreve."

"Congreve," he muttered, and again lapsed into silence. I think he was asking himself whether Congreve might be a good subject for discussion, but nothing came of this, so I made another move to get up and leave, but Moore was irritated: he was just beginning to warm up. I settled myself uncomfortably in a Louis the something chair and listened. Curiously, Moore often hesitates for the right word, and not infrequently gets it wrong. He feels for a word, and unless he is sure of it he deliberately mispronounces it, as though showing his contempt. For instance, he was speaking of an editor who commissioned him to write an article on the decay of the English language. The viewpoint suggested was the close geographical relationship between France and England. "The contig —contigunity—" Moore started, and somehow couldn't master the word *contiguity*. It is not strange that he marvelled at Bennett's facility. He even wondered, or pretended for politeness' sake to wonder, at mine, since I gave him the word he was trying to twist his tongue around; and he began to speak of my own work. He reminded me that in a recent letter I had mentioned a project to write a series of articles on the Paris of Balzac as compared with the Paris of George Moore. "I gathered that you intended to write a little book on the two subjects, which you would artfully bring together and shape into a harmonious whole. You will allow me thus to link in my mind a mountain with a molehill? I pictured you telling about a certain provincial of the time of Napoleon writing of his Paris, and some years later of another outsider doing, or trying to do, the same thing."

I answered that the idea interested me, but I had planned nothing more ambitious than perhaps two or three newspaper articles.

"Oh—I had pictured to myself a little book, and an idea was beginning to take shape in my mind. Well, if that was not your intention, don't give it another thought." For an instant he looked pained and a little puzzled: the flow of his thought was again interrupted. But he went on the next moment, waving his hands slowly. "I would gladly help you, suggest ways of going about it, furnish you material that might give color—background. I hope this is not a bad idea I have given you. My own books all came from suggestions thrown at me, or perhaps some item I had seen in a newspaper; at times the merest hint set me to thinking up a plot. *Esther Waters* took root in my mind—however, I have written all about that in one of my books, as you will recall."

"What's this you've brought me?" This sudden question he shot at me when I took from my brief-case an envelope with the title pages of several of his books; would he be good enough to sign them for me? "Of course, I'll sign anything you like. So you, too, collect books! Book-collecting is a strange passion. I used to think it a silly waste of time, but I now know that it is the collecting instinct in man that distinguishes him from the savage. Had it not been for the collectors the poems of Catullus would have been lost to us. His work was discovered in the Eighth Century by some snooping collector. In my day I have had thousands of interesting books and letters, but I kept very few of them. I gave away many, or threw them away. Very foolish, I can see.—Ah, these pages, yes. I shan't sign them now; it is late and you are tired and wish to go back to your wife, who is waiting for you, and may wish to hear whether you enjoyed your evening with me. You must be with me when I sign them, and tell me what to write. Perhaps you will come and see me soon again ? Would you care to visit the Louvre with me? Good, and when you are here I will sign the

title-pages. Next Tuesday? And I do want to meet your wife.—
No, let us postpone that pleasure to another day; she must not
come with us to see the pictures; three are too many, and our
little trip would become a party, and parties cannot look at
pictures. I am sure that is not the proper way. On Tuesday
next, then. Good night."

On the following Tuesday afternoon I called at the
Brighton. Moore was dressed in his blue serge suit, with a
strawberry pink shirt and a soft loose collar. He brought down
from his room my envelope with the title-pages, which he had
already inscribed. I began to thank him for his trouble, but he
waved me aside impatiently and drew from the same envelope the MS of a much-revised preface to the new book, *In
Single Strictness.* "Tell me honestly," he began, "how this
sounds to you." And he began reading, sonorously, slowly and
with marked emphasis: "For the unfolding of my subject more
than one story was needed; but the temperaments of the people in the stories are so closely related," etc., essentially what
was later published in the book. From what I could judge by
ear the preface ran to about a hundred and fifty words, and
seemed to be all in one sentence. He laid down the paper and
looked at me. I had little to say, so I merely complimented
him on the limpidity of the style. He scowled. He said he
wanted advice, my frank opinion, adverse criticism if I had
any to offer. But who was I to tell him how to write? Without
saying another word he read the entire preface to me again.
Now what did I think of it? I had to say something, and I ventured to suggest that it was perhaps too long for a single sentence. Why not put a period here, a semi-colon there? That
would give the reader a chance—

"It's clear, isn't it? If a long sentence is clear it is as good
as a short sentence—better. Better, I say. Without long sentences there can be no literature!" He slowly folded the paper
and with a studied frown put it into his pocket.

"Now let us go and see the pictures."

We walked across the Rue de Rivoli, and through the Tuileries Gardens. Moore asked what I had been writing that morning, and I told him of my article on Adolphe Appia.

"Appia? Appia? Oh, *that* fellow! He and Craig! Those amateurs, those incompetents in the theater, who try to conceal their intellectual barrenness by trifling with unimportant details. They fiddle around with scenery and lights and the rest of it because they can't write plays. All that really matters is the text and the acting. Why in the world do you waste your time on fellows like Appia?—Well, perhaps it is possible to write a good article, anyway. I hope yours is good. Is it?"

He would wait for no answer, now that we had come to the gates of the Louvre. His mind had gone back to our conversation of the other evening on the evils of modern education. "Everyone thinks he must needs write a novel or paint a picture, and the result of all this activity is a mess of hopeless mediocrity. My friends tell me that the system is faulty, and that I must not blame education as a thing in itself. But I tell them it must always, and necessarily, be faulty; the idea itself is wrong, for it means the moulding of all minds into the image of one mind. What in God's name will be the result of all our education? People will no longer work in the fields and dig in the mines, and then where will the rest of us be?"

"There," and pointed over his shoulder back toward the huge Gambetta statue, "that is the result of education. Frightful, meaningless! How *could* they do it? When in doubt, a sculptor puts in a nude. Senseless!" And we hurried on into the palace. "Let us forget this; there are some new acquisitions in the museum that we must not fail to see."

While we were wondering where these might be Moore paused before certain statues and pictures. Without even looking at the Niké herself, he pointed in disgust at the new mosaics that lined the inside of the niche. "Again behold the result of popular education! What a hideous thing. Who is responsible for putting the statue there? Try to find out and you will be sent from one Government official to another, and you will never learn. Never."

We paused only a moment before a few canvases in the 17th and 18th Century French rooms. "Ah, Pater! Pater was a bad painter. He—he simply didn't know his job. But here, now, Watteau's *Fête champêtre,* that is a painting. But let us not spend our time here; we must see the new acquisitions."

These were not especially striking. Here, for example, was a Berthe Morisot portrait that Moore liked. I said it reminded me of Manet, and he quoted what he had once written of her, giving Manet's own words: "Berthe Morisot has merely drawn my art across her fan."

But Manet. There was a painter. "The paint seemed to leap to his canvas. He was a painter by the grace of God.—And here are the Corots. I used to think Corot a great painter. I am off him now; I much prefer Rousseau, for Rousseau goes to the root of things, to nature herself, while Corot is—well, he is always trying to improve on nature. Let us spend no more time with Corot. I wonder; people seem to like my Héloïse, but after all isn't there more stuff, more nature, in *A Mummer's Wife?* That book was observed, through the naked eye, it was felt, and the result, by God! was life! Of course, *Héloïse* is about living men and women of today (it couldn't very well be otherwise), but it is not quite so directly, so immediately inspired by life as the early realistic book was."

Ingres, as always, aroused Moore's admiration and enthusiasm, but the Renan portrait didn't seem quite so good to him now as it did some years ago. He paused in front of the *Apotheosis of Homer,* and I told him I didn't care for it.

"No? You don't like it? But look at the figure of that angel crowning the poet. Exquisite, beautiful drawing. Yes, the grouping of the figure *is* stiff; I admit that. You are quite right; and the color is childish.—But come here and let us look at the *Olympia.* We agree on Manet, at any rate. I used to know that woman, Manet's model. This nude is alive, isn't she? The flesh lives. See that tint? Flawless. When Manet paints nudes they have meaning. Most painters just take it into their heads to paint naked women. Now, a naked woman is a very fine thing in her place and at the proper time, but I seldom care to see one in a picture. This *Olympia* is magnificent."

Much more followed on the same subject, but two small Diazes drew Moore away from Manet, as he remarked: "I would like to have those two to hang on my wall at home.— And now let us see the Rembrandts; we have had enough of the Frenchmen. Here we are—Good God! These are so badly lighted! The lighting positively kills the pictures. Who the hell is to blame for that? Some blundering official! There, that's better." Then, catching sight of the uninspired work of some follower of Rembrandt, he hissed:

"Why on earth must our museums be crowded with historical examples? It is wearisome to have to wander through room after room to find what you are looking for. Ah, here we have the Rembrandt portraits." He stood before them for a long time, but said nothing. We then passed on to the Rubens'. Moore likes only the small sketches, admires their drawing and subtle color, but he has no use for the Marie de Médicis series, "which are not Rubens at all. He may have designed them, but he never painted them. Which of these do you like best?"

I told him I admired the drawing of the man who was running, the one on the end wall. "Why, that's only the Greek gladiator we saw downstairs. Nothing original in that! Tut, tut, I had thought you a man of discrimination. Let us leave these abominable pictures." He turned quickly and with a magnificent flourish of the arm dismissed the questionable Rubens'.

We hurried on our way out, but stopped a moment in another room to look at the Fromentins. "A fine painter; as fine as a man can be who is not a great painter." And we spoke of

Fromentin's writings, Moore saying that *Dominique* was beautifully written but rather dull. I said I could not get beyond the fiftieth page and Moore answered that I had gone him better by ten pages.

"Now we have had enough art. Two hours at one time is quite sufficient. You speak of Conrad. Oh, what a very bad writer he is. Do you like him?"

By now we had left the Louvre and were slowly making our way back toward the Hotel.

"Some of his books? Which ones? Dear, dear! You disappoint me. No, I have not read *Victory* and in spite of your enthusiasm I will not read it: it cannot be good. They told me *Chance* was a fine story, so I began it, but I soon threw it aside. Let me tell you (this with a chuckle) an epigram I composed on Conrad. It's very good, I think, but perhaps a little cruel. 'Conrad is the wreckage of Stevenson floating around in the slops of Henry James.' A trifle harsh, yes, for after all Conrad did learn our language after he had grown up, and it is wonderful that he should ever have learned to write at all. He deserves credit for having attained a position in the front rank of modern English writers. But he writes very badly for a man who writes so well. He can't tell a straightforward story in a straightforward way. Such involved and turgid sentences!"

From Conrad he led the talk around to another of his pet literary aversions, Thomas Hardy. "Have I told you my epigram on Hardy? 'One of George Eliot's miscarriages.' Now, Hardy cannot write at all, and his machine-made plots are mawkish and absurd. See how he drags in trivial and unessential scenes in order to make use of that stage moonlight of his! I was reading *Tess of the*—er—that Tess book when I was working on *Esther Waters*. Compare the two books, I ask you! I recall an absurd scene where the man (what's his name?) carries Tess over the plain at night. Moonlight, naturally! Of course I thought he was going to take her to his room, put her in bed and get in beside her. A happy ending was obviously what he was leading up to, but that is not what we get. Something irrelevant was thrust into the narrative—one of those damn mechanical plot turns, and nothing happened at all. The fellow did nothing with the girl! Oh, Hardy is a shockingly bad writer. Why doesn't someone say that? Why don't you write an article on him, proving that the man can't write English? You could begin by saying that 'Thomas Hardy enjoys the reputation of—' but no, I suppose you wouldn't care to do it? No."

He stopped right there in the middle of the Tuileries Gardens, looking soberly at me as he twisted his white moustache, wondering perhaps how much of what he was saying impressed me. I allowed him to go on, and as we started walking again, he spoke of Stevenson.

"His novels don't appeal to me. They are little more than children's toys, but the travel books and essays are very fine. They criticize Stevenson nowadays for being an artificial writer. I can't see the reason for that at all. Flaubert, on the other hand, is not so good a writer as I used to think him. Ten years ago I realized that he was not a great writer, and when I said so nobody believed me. Today everyone admits I was right."

Halted in the middle of the traffic on the Rue de Rivoli Moore stopped short and asked whether I had been able to settle the *Jurgen* case, as though I had myself been judge and jury in the trial that had shortly before aroused something of a controversy in America. I told him, meanwhile urging him to safety across the street, that a superior court had reversed the earlier verdict against Cabell.

"So there *are* some sane and sensible people in your country! I knew that, of course, but I hardly suspected there were enough to get together and wage effective battle against the—what do you call them? The smut-hounds? I liked *Jurgen*, but I don't think I saw in it all the fine things you tell me about. I hope the book will sell well now, for it is an honest and intelligent work."

"I don't think the author will care to re-issue it just now," I said, for I remembered Cabell telling me of his disgust over the pother, hinting that he might withdraw the book permanently.

"What do you mean?", asked Moore. "Why in the world would he do that?"

"People might read the book just for the real, or alleged, smut."

"If the man thinks that he's a fool. Tell Mr. Cabell that from me. What does he care why people read his books? If I inquired into all the motives of *my* readers—! Good God, suppose they do read *Jurgen* for the smut? People like smut; if it's good smut, all the better. I suppose my *Story-Teller's Holiday* is read for its smut. I haven't the least objection to that. I like smut. It is good for one. Why not?"

We had now reached the Brighton, and Moore left me in the lobby while he went upstairs to bring down the signed title pages I had given him. From among these he drew forth a reproduction of one of Jacques Blanche's portraits of him. "No," he shouted, throwing the picture on to a desk, "I won't sign that for you. Look at it! That's Blanche all over, putting himself, all of himself and nothing of the sitter onto the canvas. I once offended Blanche by telling him that he had made me look like a drunken London cabby. I spoke only the plain truth—maybe that's why Blanche didn't like my remark? By the way, Blanche must have a great many of my early books. If you are interested, go and see him. Do that; he is a pleasant enough fellow. And there must be many others who have early letters of mine, and what you call 'presentation copies.' Get in touch with the heirs of Mme. Bouguereau; I wrote about her in my books under the name of Lizzie Gardiner; she is in *Memoirs of My Dead Life* and *Avowals.*—My mistress nearly fifty years ago. I used to send her all my books. Go at once to her apartment and offer the concierge something; it need not be much—fifteen or twenty francs, perhaps. There is a chance you may find something. It would be interesting to see. You don't care to? Suit yourself. And now let us take a little walk; a stroll under these stone arcades will be an agreeable change. You have time?" I had, and we ambled along, stopping at two or three book-shops. Friends had recommended new French books, which Moore bought. He spoke a somewhat fluent, stiff, stagey and often incorrect French. He stood, umbrella tucked under one arm, reading one of his new purchases. The flow of reminiscence and conversation had suddenly stopped short, and I knew it was time for me to leave. As I went out he was standing motionless, reading, a remotely comical old gentleman, all curves and suave lines, with hardly a trace of stomach; large soft hands, white flowing moustache. A loosely-constructed framework. As I went out the shop door he looked up gravely, with a tiny smile, as though saying, "Are you still here?"

Moore had meantime returned to London, and toward the end of April I wrote saying I had given serious thought to his suggestion that we work together on a new version of the *Esther Waters* play. On the 20th he replied:

> Your letter has just come to hand and it so happens that you can do me a favour. I should like to start for Paris Saturday morning but unless I can get a room I shall have to postpone my departure till next week. A friend has been to the Hotel Voltaire, to the Hotel du Pas de Calais and to the Hotel des Sts Peres but has not been able to telegraph anything definite. She tells me she has engaged a room above Foyot's restaurant but I went there once and had to leave the next morning so great was the noise. I cannot go back to the abominable Brighton. If you succeed in getting me a suitable room will you write or better still telegraph.
>
> *Sincerely yours.*

This came on a Saturday, and acting on the advice of someone who knew Cayre's Hotel in the Rue du Bac I engaged a room there and sent a wire to Moore. Next morning, as usual, I went to the Deux Magots to work. For some reason, doubtless connected with the *Esther Waters* project, I had taken with me a copy of *Memoirs of My Dead Life*. It was about eleven, and as I was making some notation in the book I half looked up and caught sight out of the tail of my eye of two figures standing before me, Cecile and Moore. Cecile said she had brought a friend to see me, and Moore broke into a broad grin.

As Cecile explained to me later, Moore had come to our attic room in the Rue Visconti while she was washing the breakfast dishes. Hearing the knock on the door she had a premonition that the caller was Moore. When she invited him in she called him by name.

"My dear young lady, how did you know who I was?" He came in and sat on the couch.

"I've seen pictures of you, and besides, when Barrett and I were passing your hotel some weeks ago I peeked into the writing room and saw you. Barrett's not in now."

"Then I have come to take *you* out to breakfast."

"I think he's at the Deux Magots. He works there nearly every morning."

"Suppose we didn't go there, or went and missed him, would you give me the pleasure of taking *you* alone to breakfast? He wouldn't divorce you for that, would he?"

"No, not for *that*. Suppose we go now? I have to get ready."

"How long will that take?"

"Not a minute."

As Cecile was putting on her things in our makeshift kitchen Moore settled himself comfortably in one of our old chairs and picked up the book Cecile had been reading, Walter de la Mare's *Memoirs of a Midget*. "Do you like this? What do you think of it? I know de la Mare. I thought the first few chapters were very good, but I couldn't finish the rest. Tell me now—I'm surprised and delighted you got ready so soon— why didn't you stop in at the Hotel the day you peeped at me, and introduce yourself? You surely wouldn't run away from a staid old gentleman like me?"

Moore insisted that they take a taxi, though the café was only three minutes' walk from our room. In the taxi Moore burst into a flood of questions: "So this is your first visit to Paris? How do you like it? What are your impressions? Are you enjoying yourself? Will you learn French? You are just the right age to learn. Tell me—"

As the taxi drove up to the Deux Magots, Moore stepped out lightly and offered his arm.

"Your husband won't think I'm trying to run off with you, will he?"

"I think he'd be flattered if you were."

"Oh no, my dear, not with an old man like me!"

We sat for a few minutes at my table. Moore took his place on the edge of a chair and sat there motionless and erect. After refusing coffee, he leaned over in my direction and asked what I was doing. I showed him the *Memoirs*. "Good literature," I commented, but he lost his smile.

"That awful book! Yes, even in the Heinemann edition! The only decent edition is the new one. Don't read it in any other, promise me that."

When I found we could not get a regular breakfast at the Deux Magots we went next door to the Café de Flore, and *au premier* ordered a large meal for Moore, while Cecile and I took coffee. We sat there at an open window looking down the Boulevard St. Germain, where the buds on the trees were just beginning to break open. Moore tried to induce us to order a real meal, but as we had breakfasted not long before, we refused.

"When do you eat your breakfast? It's early now." It was way past eleven, we said, and when Moore doubted that I showed him my watch. Dear dear! He was a trifle irritated: he wants things to turn out just as he plans them.

As usual, Moore talked a great deal about trivial matters:

how the French fry bacon; hotel rooms and service; the birds in the trees along the Boulevards. But from these trivialities he drifted into literature, the arts, philosophy.

Reverting to *Memoirs of My Dead Life,* he declared that the book had been gathered together out of stray articles and stories. "That was no proper way to make a book, and the *Memoirs* in consequence lacks unity. In the new edition I have striven to give it some sort of artistic direction.—You will be amused, I think, with the frontispiece, a colored photograph of myself as a boy of five. I have given the book a touch of rouge, which makes the whole world kin." He smiled as he told us it had taken him a long time to shape and polish off that epigram.

"Oh, now I must tell you about the hotel room. It's a long story—if you don't mind? Lady Cunard's daughter, Nancy, got me a room at Foyot's. As I wrote you, I was afraid that place was going to be too noisy; as a matter of fact it is, but when I arrived last night in the pouring rain I went there at once, intending to go on to Cayre's. But in my room was a large bouquet of forget-me-nots the young lady had sent in for me. If it had not been for those flowers I would have gone to the other place; but how could I resist the forget-me-nots? You see, my dear (this to Cecile) I'm a sentimental old man.—Foyot's is dreadfully expensive, especially the food. That's why I didn't ask you there to breakfast. It would have cost me two or three hundred francs." He smiled benignly, but we couldn't make out whether he was serious or not. I think he was.

Moore now asked Cecile more questions: How she liked the theater in Paris; whether she enjoyed the Louvre; how long we planned to stay; and he was most particular in urging her to learn the language. "It's not at all hard, but you must first learn a few verbs; you cannot speak a language without verbs. There are only very few that are basically necessary. See how simple they are—This one, of course, is the commonest and incidentally the most useful—*J'aime, tu aimes, il aime, tu aimeras*, etc. And you needn't be afraid of not speaking it well. I don't. Even your husband here doesn't, though I am sure his French is better than mine; no foreigner ever speaks it perfectly, and few, very few Frenchmen."

"But you, Mr. Moore," I said, "speak it with some facility, though, as you say, you haven't lived in France for many years."

"My French," he answered, "is not precisely the French of today. I learned the language from Verlaine and Mallarmé, Zola and Manet and the others."

"But now let us change the subject and speak of our play, unless you care to defer this until our next meeting?" I thought it best to discuss the matter now: I was ready to begin work. The rest of our session was devoted to this matter, though we constantly jumped from the play to Balzac, the condition of the theater, the disappearance of the old-time cocotte, and popular education. Inasmuch as our collaboration on *Esther Waters* is best related consecutively I shall tell that story as though our many subsequent talks and meetings centered only on that one subject. The story will begin at the end of my relation of this morning's visit at the Café de Flore.

Moore complained of the many bad plays he had seen recently in London, and he emphasized in particular the scenery and stage direction. But he had been impressed by the charm and talent of a new English actress, Athene Seiler, who was anxious to play the leading role in his comedy *The Coming of Gabrielle*. "She came to my home for dinner not long ago. A wonderful woman, and a marvelous listener. She acts with her face, her arms, with the tips of her boots; even with the hem of her skirt. Kathleen Nesbitt had tried to see what she could do with the role, but she was awful! Quite out of the question. The play was already in rehearsal, but when I saw her act I withdrew it, declaring that the whole cast was unsatisfactory. It was a reason, at any rate, and one must always give a reason, though in this case it was not literally the true reason. For example, when you break off an affair with a woman you give your reason, though you cannot tell the true one, which is simply that you have ceased to love her. In my case I had ceased to love one actress, and fallen in love with another."

Speaking of the style of *The Brook Kerith*, Moore told how a few days ago he had read parts of the original edition, and had been shocked by the modernisms. These, he said, threw the book out of key. "There are entire passages that make my blood run cold. In one place someone asks whether a certain man has 'business capacity'? Dreadful. Imagine saying that! I changed the expression to 'fit for trade.' The novel was written too hurriedly, and it was inevitable that such things should creep in. That is why I am always revising my early books. You know I am at work on a collected edition of my writings for Liveright in America? *Impressions and Opinions* is to be dismembered, many of the essays discarded, some rewritten, and some put into other books. The paper on Balzac is very bad; that I am rewriting entirely. There was a passage from Balzac I wanted to quote in it, but it was so carelessly and obscurely written—I mean by Balzac himself—that my literal translation meant nothing at all. What should I do about that, I wondered? Leave it out entirely? I tried my hand at it and made four or five versions and at last, with the help of my secretary, I achieved something very fine. It's only a short passage, an epigram, or what Balzac intended as an epigram."

"What did you do with the original?" I asked. "Read between the lines?"

"What? What lines?" He didn't get me!

I motioned to him to proceed with his story, for it was plain I had interfered with the flow of his thought, and he doesn't like that. His lips puckered into what may have been intended as a smile: I could not be sure.

"I said what Balzac had meant to say what he had not taken the trouble to express clearly enough. He wrote so fast in the first place that he had to do the greater part of his work on his galley proofs. The epigram I made out of his words is not really his own, and I am in doubt whether to ascribe it to him or to myself. Here it is, and I think it's rather good: 'One touch of rouge makes vice attractive.' "

Speaking of the *Contes drolatiques* Moore claimed that they are in many ways Balzac's finest achievement. "Writing in what is supposed to be 16th Century French, Balzac was forced to discipline himself; he was extremely careful; he showed unusual discrimination in his composition and style. He couldn't so easily wander into the byways of philosophy as he did in his modern books. The stories are beautifully constructed and written, and vastly amusing, as you know. I am not scholar enough to determine just what style he was using; perhaps a composite, in which 16th Century predominates. A recent translation of some of the stories is written in an English so old and obscure (and doubtless authentic) that I can't make head nor tail out of it."

"In one way, my *Héloïse and Abélard* was a similar literary exercise. But that book is modern, both in spirit and mood. I am now going through the text again, cutting out everything that would make the reader think I was striving after the archaic, yet I am keeping nothing that is distinctively modern. In fact I aim to make the style a kind of composite of modern and 18th Century English."

Reverting, as he constantly does, to the new collected edition of his works, he spoke of the general preface he is now working on. From some new American friend (Chew, I think) he had heard much about the Southeastern American mountain folk, and intended to make some reference to them in his preface. Cecile told him that she knew a good deal about the Maryland and Virginia country people, with whom she had lived when she taught school near Hancock. Moore was at once on the alert. He asked all sorts of questions about their habits and clothes and speech, and Cecile told about McCusker the outlaw, who lived in a cave in the Blue Ridge for some years, a woman secretly bringing him food and clothing. When Cecile had done Moore asked whether he might use the story as she told it, "attributing it to my other friend, who is already introduced into the narrative as I have started to write it? It would not do to interrupt the story by bringing you in, too.—Good. Now I shall win a high reputation among American readers for my exact knowledge of your mountain people. But tell me more about that woman.—Yes, yes. It is wonderful, there is always a woman ready to do that kind of thing for a man, no matter how ugly or repulsive he may be. A woman was inevitable in your story, and she shall have a place in mine."

"But my dear young lady, we are perhaps boring you with all this talk about books? You are a musician; now tell me about your work. The piano? Dear, dear, the piano is a vile instrument, impossible as a medium for true musical expression. I used to know Paderewski intimately; the struggles that poor fellow had to get anything at all out of his instrument!—I am sorry. Music I know and care very little about—I mean the new music. It is like almost everything new in literature and painting; but I daresay I am too old to appreciate it. I am beginning to think there is already enough art in the world, at least for my taste, so why should I go to the trouble of trying to make head or tail of the new? Do *you* see anything in it? Perhaps I am missing some fresh experience, but I have enough now, and if I am able to make new friends (people are always interesting) I shall not complain."

"But don't you remember the first time you heard Wagner?"

"Yes, yes, I see the direction of your argument, young man, and I confess that *Rheingold* meant nothing to me at the first, nor even at the second hearing. Then I heard *Tristan,* and the second time I heard that I became a confirmed Wagnerian. Yet today I find I can get along very well even without Wagner. Thus do our tastes change."

Yet it was clear that Moore does manage to keep abreast of much that is new, in art, literature, and music. He is always telling us of some new exhibition of paintings he has attended, or a new play in the theater.

"Perhaps we have talked enough now, unless you would care to discuss *Esther Waters;* but before we do that I should like to ask you both to dine with me some time later in the week."

"I think," Cecile ventured, "you and Barrett might prefer to be alone."

"Don't you *want* to dine with me?" He looked very grave, and asked the question with some petulance.

"Surely I *want* to."

"Then let us hear no more about your husband and me dining alone together. You will both come to Foyot's Tuesday evening. The Hotel, I mean, not the restaurant."

A propos of nothing at all that I remember, Moore spoke of his book of Irish essays, of which I had just bought a French translation under the title *Terre d'Irlande*, and remarked ruefully that he had been unfortunate in his translators. "But let us say nothing more about that wretched book and my translators. Tell me, are there any good restaurants near Foyot's? I can't afford to eat there. The Voltaire? Is it good? After we leave here you may show me the Voltaire."

We were now ready to talk about *Esther Waters*.

In a very literal sense Moore's life has been a long series of collaborations. Though he has devoted many pages of melodious prose to a recital of his more picturesque ventures in quest of literary material, there are other anecdotes, especially connected with his attempts to write plays, that ought to be related. No one who knows the man can question his honesty, and I am sure he would not willingly conceal facts about himself, so long as they are interesting and make good copy. Moore has never scrupled to rearrange facts in the history of his own career or in the careers of his friends, and he has from the beginning made generous use of other people's ideas. Henry James, unjustly I think, called him a picker of other men's brains. *Je prends mon bien partout où je le trouve.* Moore has made use of what he took quite as skilfully and as legitimately as Molière, and our quarrel with him is surely not over his borrowings. Indeed, we have no quarrel at all. My only excuse for jotting down these notes is a desire to record the literal truth about the one collaboration in which I shared.

Nearly all of Moore's dramatic experiments were collaborations. In fairness to him I must say that sooner or later he rejected most of the suggestions made to him. Dujardin once told me that Moore used to send him French sentences for correction, but that in the final proofs the corrections were nowhere to be found.

After almost fifty years of experiment Moore still believed he could write a good play, and no one could ever convince him that pretty writing is not the first requisite of effective drama. To this day, in spite of his acute critical sense, he judges most plays by their literary qualities. Yet all his own plays are potentially dramatic. *The Coming of Gabrielle* was begun many years ago, and now, under its third title, it is no better than when it appeared originally as *Elizabeth Cooper:* years of collaboration with Dujardin and the criticism of countless friends seem to have done nothing to help the play.

Moore's plays are, as I have said, the result of collaboration. Dujardin and others labored for years on *The Peacock's Feathers* (now *The Coming of Gabrielle*); Martyn supplied the first story for *The Bending of the Bough;* Lopez was the (acknowledged) part author of *Martin Luther;* Arthur Kennedy's name appears jointly with Moore's on one manuscript of *The Strike at Arlingford;* the first version of the dramatization of *Esther Waters* owes something to an unnamed "very intelligent young man," and the final version of the same play contains something of my own; John Balderston made a scenario of *The Brook Kerith,* of which *The Apostle* was the outcome.

Just when and how the first dramatization of the novel *Esther Waters* was made, I have not been able to discover. One version was begun as early as 1910, for I found in one of Moore's letters to Dujardin a reference to the "very intelligent young man" who is working at it. Moore is "very sure" he will produce "excellent results." The play, with no mention of the young man, was produced by the London Stage Society in 1912 and printed in book form in 1913.

I got hold of a copy of the novel and the play, and when Moore next came to Paris we were ready for work. Two months after our first discussion we breakfasted at the Café de Flore on the Boulevard St. Germain.

"Well," he began before we were seated, "what do you think about our *Esther Waters?*"

I told him I believed the first two acts might stand practically as written, but that the last two were bad. About the third I was uncertain. The first two followed the novel almost literally, but the third foreshadowed a melodramatic situation which was out of key with the rest.

"We shall need a new third act," said Moore, "and the last two must be dropped. The present third can be revised and used as the last act of the new play we are going to write. There is no reason why we should not have a conventional happy ending. It doesn't destroy the artistic unity of the story, and it will help make it a commercial success. You are right in saying that the present five-act version is much too long. It will never do."

"There is one point, Mr. Moore, I should like to raise."

"What point?"

"I have always thought that Esther's meeting with William, an incident on which all the rest depends (I speak of the play, of course, not the novel), is entirely too casual; it is brought about by a coincidence. William, I think, ought to have been looking for Esther, wanting her, still loving her. Their meeting is purely fortuitous. Now, I think—"

"No, no," he interrupted with a scowl, "that's life. It must be casual. You are seeking to make it mechanical. That's just the way things happen in life."

"But all the subsequent action is made to depend on a pure coincidence."

"Yes, yes, but that's the way things happen."

"In life, perhaps, and to a certain extent in novels, but in plays is it not true that you must have a quick succession of cause and effect, leaving nothing (or almost nothing) to chance? Don't you believe that the dramatist must make his points clear?"

Moore laid down knife and fork with a touch of annoyance. "But my dear young man, you want to tie all the strings! Do you want to write a Scribe play?"

We got no further on this point, and I thought it wise to direct Moore's attention to the new third act. Though he was afraid I was over-anxious to bolster up the plot by what I deemed necessary **logic** rather than "life," he invited me to undertake with him the re-writing of the play. There was no reason, he thought, why a good play should not succeed on the contemporary stage.

"These 'successful' managers! They produce a dozen stupid plays that fail, and persist in refusing good plays. Is that why they are called successful? They say of a good play, 'No, the public wants this and doesn't want that,' but what the hell do they know about it? I don't say I can choose a play that is sure to make a tremendous success, but I can certainly tell whether it would fail instantly, or have a fair chance of success."

Some days afterward we dined at the Voltaire, a quiet old restaurant opposite the Odéon. It had been agreed that Moore was to put down his ideas on the general form of the new third act, and submit to me an agreement covering our collaboration. At the same time I was to write out my own ideas, and when we should have agreed on the outline I was to go ahead and re-write the play. Moore had already made his notes for the new act, and these he read to me as we were waiting to be served. The new act was to begin with the coming of Esther's former employer, Mrs. Barfield, to the home of Miss Rice, where Esther was in service. Esther is by now fairly happy, as she is able to support her little boy, and she has apparently forgotten her handsome seducer, William. The incident of the broken beer jug, described at length in the novel, was then to be introduced as a device to bring about the meeting between Esther and William. This was, of course, to happen off-stage. Meantime Mrs. Barfield and Miss Rice discuss Esther and Esther's fiancé, Fred Parsons. Toward the end of the scene Esther enters, very much upset. It is clear that the reappearance of William has stirred up old memories and that she is still in love with him.

"The end of the act," said Moore, as he laid down his notes, "might be Esther going to fetch William, and Miss Rice left waiting on the stage."

Though the "scenario" was brief and indicated only the general trend of the action, it seemed satisfactory to us both.

"Very well, then," said Moore, "I'll have this copied and sent to you, and you may go ahead and write it out. Use this outline if you can or throw it aside if you don't want it.—Whatever you think best. And if you like—though I advise you to do only one thing at a time—introduce any changes you wish in the other acts. I am sure we shall have wonderful success with our play: I can see it now in its completed form, a far better play than the old one. I hope we shall make a great deal of money. I shall print the new version in one of the volumes

of my collected edition that is to appear in America, together
with *The Coming of Gabrielle* and a one-act play about Shakespeare that I intend to finish later on. But let us agree now
that only my name is to appear in the printed edition. You
understand that? It would be unwise for both our names to go
on the title-page. You shall of course receive full credit on the
manuscript and the program in case the play is produced. This
should be clear now, for we must avoid a quarrel. I am sure I
should never dream of quarrelling with you, but we shall pre-
vent misunderstandings if we make a written agreement. I
will write you and you will send me an answer.—And now to
business.

"I have thought over what you said last time about the
coincidental meeting of Esther and William. I still think I am
right, but I see that that incident must be somewhat ex-
panded. You can do that when you write the act. You should
have no difficulty, I believe: you can do the act in a week—
there is no more than a week's work in it. When you finish it
you can send it to me at Fontainebleau and I shall look over it
there. But not for a week, I beg you, because I shall be busy
writing the Preface for my Collected Works. Liveright in worrying me for the Ms, and I suppose I must satisfy him."

We had finished dinner and strolled back to Foyot's
through the narrow streets beyond the Odéon, the fading
light of an April evening turning the old plaster façades of the
tall houses to a mellow orange. I stood uneasily in the courtyard of the aged hostelry, for I imagined that Moore was tired
of talking, but I did not yet know that conversation was his
chief delight. The evening was just beginning for him, and
he insisted on my coming up to his room. He was "following
the line" of his thought, as he put it, and to interrupt him at
such a time is to court the dreaded Moorish frown. The rest of
the evening was spent in discussing the technique of novels,
the fatuousness of Zola, the proper mode of address to a discarded mistress, American censorship, and the decay of paint-

ing. It was long after midnight when Moore came downstairs with me. We waked the concierge by offering him a gratuity, and I started down the Rue de Tournon, turning back a moment later in response to Moore's remark that I "must not make the play too mechanical!"

Toward the end of the week I got back from him the scenario for the third act, together with a letter setting forth the conditions of our collaboration. I was to "turn" the scenario "into dialogue," and Moore was to "rewrite the dialogue, for as we agreed, the play cannot be in two styles." William was to be accepted by Esther at the end of the play, because Esther is no longer able to "stand the strain" of living without him. I was to try to sell the manuscript in America, in which case it was to be signed by both of us, but if it were played in London, by Moore alone. In any event I was to receive half the royalties from all stage performances.

These terms I accepted and at once set to work. When it came to "turning the scenario into dialogue," the process was not so easy as Moore had imagined. I therefore wrote a new act in which I showed briefly what had happened since the curtain fell on the second act, an interval of six years. I also added to the dialogue between Miss Rice and Mrs. Barfield a good deal of necessary information about Fred Parsons, whom I intended to introduce into the last act, otherwise the audience would have to take for granted the bald statement that Esther had thrown over her fiancé. I wanted to show the two men together. Finally, I furnished Esther with sufficient motive for behaving as she does, all mention of which was omitted from Moore's outline, and gave the act what I considered a dramatic curtain. I then went through the other three acts, all of which had to be modified in order to fit in with the third, and to incorporate certain matters that were left over from the old fourth and fifth acts. I cut perhaps twenty-five pages of the original dialogue, added a speech or a line here and there, and completely changed the end of each act.

I then sent Moore the new act, the corrected text of the whole play, and notes explaining my reasons for each step in the work I had done. Two days later I received a letter from Fontainebleau. It was useless, Moore said, to write a long letter, which would only "perplex and mystify" me; he would like to talk the matter over; would I not therefore come to him? Perhaps Mrs. Clark would also give him the pleasure of her company? We should have lunch and afterward we could "go into the dramatic question" in the garden. On second thought, the garden would not do: the "room I am writing to you from would doubtless be more appropriate."

Two days afterward I arrived, alone, at the Fontainebleau station in a pouring rain. Moore had walked all the way from the villa through the mud to offer me the shelter of his umbrella! Ah, so Mrs. Clark was not with me? Too bad, too bad! "I had pictured her sitting in the garden, if the day had been pleasant, while we worked together on our play. But I daresay it is better she did not come. The garden would be detestable, and it is not pleasant to sit indoors on a spring day."

At Le Val Changis I was perfunctorily introduced to the amiable Dujardin, and then hurried upstairs to Moore's bedroom.

"I thought it wisest," he began at once, "to bring you down here. Otherwise we might never have come to an understanding. We would have exchanged long letters and very possibly have arrived nowhere in the end. Sit down now and let me see what you have done.

"I am very well satisfied with the first half of the new act. That is splendid. But you fail utterly after Esther's entrance. I didn't read any further. I couldn't."

"But," I ventured to interrupt, "do you mean that the entrance itself is so shocking that the rest of the act couldn't possibly be good?"

"I only glanced at the rest, but it was not necessary to do

(97)

even that. You start Esther off reasoning; you kill the whole damned act—I mean the last part of it."

I again reminded Moore that it was necessary to motivate Esther's actions, and at that strategic point prepare not only for the scene to follow, but for the end of the whole play, the happy end we had agreed on. "Don't you see," I began, "she must have reasons, and the audience must understand—"

"My dear young friend, you want to reason the whole damned play out of existence! You are always giving reasons. The audience don't want reasons, they want drama. Esther is a woman of emotions, strong feelings, passions. People of her class don't reason. No, no, you are on the wrong track. You see, she must simply come in, after dropping the jug, burst into the room, and there you are!"

"But, Mr. Moore, that will reduce our act to about five minutes of dialogue before Esther's entrance. When Esther comes in, if she is only to feel, you have no act at all. You can't have Maeterlinck's old man sitting before a fire, you know—at least in this sort of play—"

Moore's eyes glazed over. "What are you talking about? Maeterlinck—Maeterlinck?—Of course Esther says something: she relates the incident of the jug, blurting it out incoherently. Her whole life is finished, she says, and there's the end of your act. But if you insist on making the rest of the scene a long argument, with reasons and all, you'll have no last act whatsoever."

"Passion, Mr. Moore, is all very well. I wish I could put it over better than I have done (I must leave that to you!), but after all, Esther is not an animal. She isn't that in your novel, and even if she can't reason things out herself or clearly express her mental processes, such as they are, the audience must realize *why* she behaves as she does." But I was talking to thin air, for Moore was following the line of his thought.

He rose from his chair at the table and began pacing before the open window:

"I must get the tone of the scene," he said, and kept repeating, " the tone, that is what we must have. Let me see," and he waved his hand gracefully, describing circles, as his blue eyes lighted up again. "Now, now I have it, I think! I can't give you the exact words, but this is—this is the proper tone—

. "And then Miss Rice tells her 'Here is your friend Mrs. Barfield, Esther,' and Esther says, 'Yes Miss,' and then she sobs and Mrs. Barfield says, 'Tell us Esther what's the matter.' 'Oh I couldn't Ma'am I really couldn't it's all too dreadful Ma'am.' 'But what's too dreadful Esther we can't help you if you don't tell us what's the matter.' 'Oh I couldn't oh I'm so sorry Miss' and so on and so on." Speech rolled out after speech without punctuation, but with a majestic rhythm accentuated by broad sweeping gestures. Moore tasted each word lingeringly as it fell from his lips, enjoying the deep sonority of his resonant voice.

"There you are," he said with satisfaction, "those are not the precise words, but you have the tone of the scene. And then Miss Rice might rise and go over to Esther, and there you have your scene. Now let me see what else you have done." He sat down again and took up the manuscript.

"What's this? What have you done here? Ah, yes. Well, that's all right, but what's the matter with this speech? Why have you cut it out? What didn't you like? Oh—oh! Yes—yes, that's good. I should never have thought of that. Now here, in all this first part of the act you have done very nicely. I see you've introduced a reference to Fred—what's his name? Fred Parsons, yes. That was necessary. Good! Yes, the first fifteen pages are first-rate. They could hardly be better. Naturally, I think I can improve the style here and there. Occasionally your expressions are not English. Here's an Americanism. Mrs. Barfield would never say 'a sip of tea,' but that is a detail. Nor would she think of kissing Esther. Dear, no! But almost all your dialogue may stand just as it is."

He now trotted over to the far end of the room, his silky

white hair streaming in the breeze that blew in through the window. He stood there perplexed. The tone of the scene had once more eluded us.—Ah, it comes at last!

"Now, let me see if we can't get the tone of the rest of that act."

And once more he began to cut great circles in the air, chanting dialogue and rolling his R's. But scarcely had the elusive tone been captured when we were interrupted by the cheery voice of Dujardin below, announcing lunch. Moore's arms fell limply and he muttered a long curse.

"God damn it, are we never to be free from interruptions! I suppose we must go down to lunch now.—We've lost the tone! Let us hope we shall find it again. But we'll come up immediately after lunch." And we did, unceremoniously leaving the company at coffee.

It was not easy to recapture that tone.

"I almost had it," said Moore ruefully, looking like Don Quixote after a misadventure, "when we were called to lunch! Now tell me," he continued, sitting down opposite me, "I don't want to force my ideas on you: tell me frankly if you don't agree with me. You may, if you like, go ahead with your own version and send it to America as it now stands; you may sign it yourself, call it your own play, 'adapted from the novel of George Moore.' I really don't care a damn. But I advise you not to do that. I am sure it wouldn't be accepted. By making Esther a reasonable and reasoning girl and explaining all her motives and thoughts, you will certainly spoil the play. I'm not even considering it from a literary viewpoint: I'm thinking of the average audience. If you are not careful you will ruin the whole bloody thing. Remember, people want emotion, feeling, not analysis. You analyze too much. Don't say you agree with me if you don't."

"I agree with you on general principles. Your theory is quite right. Emotion is, of course, what the audience wants and emotion explains nearly all of Esther's acts, but somehow we must understand her emotions. It's all right for Lear or Othello to be as emotional as they like, but we, the audience, must know why."

"We are talking about Esther, so why drag in Shakespeare?"

"I was trying to illustrate my point, Mr. Moore. To resume: Esther (you make this clear in the novel) is religious, she is a 'good girl,' and she would not throw over Fred Parsons for William without thinking a great deal about it. She has a conscience, and having a conscience implies some sort of reasoning power. Let us at least have her reasons—"

"Damn her reasons! We don't want reasons! The girl loves one man and she doesn't love the other. What better reasons do you want?"

"True, but I think you forget that since the close of act two, six years have gone by, and we must know a little of what had happened to Esther during that time, mustn't we?"

But my argument got nowhere. Moore was seeking a new line of thought and his eyes went dull again. A moment later he rose and with fresh animation began once more his elliptical gesticulations. A flood of dialogue poured forth. "There is the way the scene should go," was the peroration of his remarks, which had followed much the same course as the speech he made before lunch.

We now turned to my revisions in the original printed text. The second act, laid in the home of the baby-farmer, Mrs. Spires, ends abruptly after the entrance of the collector Fred Parsons. I had developed the scene, showing Esther succumbing to the fascination of the attractive stranger, and had decided to make Esther's choice between him and William the basis of an important scene later in the play. Esther's religious scruples were to be used as the motive for her increased interest in the devout Plymouth Brother. Since Esther is to be engaged to him in the third act, I thought it wise to "plant" this preparatory incident in the second.

The new scene won Moore's unqualified approval. "Just right," he said, and turned to the first pages of the same act. He was curious to see what cuts I had made. He scrutinized each alteration, and on reaching the original end of the act he smiled. There had been a long soliloquy there spoken by Mrs. Spires, and this I had entirely cut out.

"I suppose you, an up-to-date young man, would consider yourself eternally damned if you had allowed my soliloquy to stand? Don't bother to explain, my dear friend: I daresay you are right. The soliloquy was bad, I see that. Yes, yes, the new end is splendid.—But what's this?" He stopped short, his eyebrows arched. He took up his pen and deleted two of my new speeches. These were to end the act as I had written it. Mrs. Spires, seeing Esther go out with Fred, whispers to the girl, "Old onto 'im, dearie, you don't find 'em every day!," to which Esther replies, "You wicked old thing!" Not an inspiration, I admit.

"Oh, dear! Oh, dear!" sighed Moore, "that's awful. 'You wicked old thing!' Why, the audience would laugh and your whole act would be ruined." I defended the speech by saying that Esther, being rather naive, would probably have used that very expression. "As a matter of fact, Mr. Moore, you yourself put into her mouth very much the same sort of thing."

"I! Oh, no, never in the world! She would never say anything like that." I then turned to the following speech, earlier in the scene: "You wicked woman! Oh, this is awful!" Moore admits this was bad, "but not so bad as yours!," he added with a smile.

I had also cut eight pages from the first act, including the long speeches about horse-racing, and I made a new ending. Likewise I had questioned the advisability of having Mrs. Barfield kneel and pray with Esther. To these cuts Moore agreed, but insisted that when the play was acted a few years ago the prayer scene was effective in the theater.

To the new fourth act (the old third act re-written) I had

added much new material, especially a long scene where Fred and William face each other. This was done to keep up the suspense begun in the preceding act, and to introduce the sort of scene that always goes in the theater, where a woman is forced to choose between two men. Had I acted on Moore's suggestion about the third act, there would have been no fourth, and a fourth was necessary to show the development of Esther's character in accordance with what we know of it from the first part of the play.

Somehow Moore would not comment at length on the scene between the two men, though he did murmur that it seemed dramatic; but the moment we came to the scene where Esther is called upon to reveal the struggle going on between her longing for William and her sense of duty toward Fred, who has saved her and her boy, I was accused of having "intellectualized too damn much":

"Here," said Moore, rapidly turning over the leaves, "here is more discussion, when all you want is passion. Esther doesn't argue, she takes William back because he says nice things to her and holds her tight in his arms, reminds her of 'that soft night on the Downs, Esther, when you said you loved me,' and so on, and finally because he is Jackie's father, and that's all there is to it."

"But passion, Mr. Moore, that is dumb, cannot be made—"

"Oh, suit yourself, my friend, do what you like with the play! But I know these characters better than you do—that's only natural—and I think my suggestions may help you. Do you agree?"

"I know you haven't asked me to do this work just to have me say Yes to all your suggestions. If that is what you wanted you might have dictated the play to suit yourself. I think it best to go ahead with 'my' version and at the same time write another that satisfies you. Anyway, let me hear all you have to say."

"The trouble with us all," he went on, "is that we will not allow our characters to be their own natural selves. We over-write them; we are constantly over-writing. Shakespeare ruined Falstaff—that speech about honor in *Henry IV* is entirely out of character. It's Shakespeare and not Falstaff. Sancho Panza in the First Part of *Don Quixote* is marvelous, but in the Second Part Cervantes intellectualizes him. Reasons, you see, motives, analysis, explanation! They all do it, from Shakespeare and Cervantes to Moore and Clark. *I* am constantly doing it. I think the only time I was entirely successful in leaving a character absolutely alone was when I wrote the fat man in *A Mummer's Wife*. He is very good. My God, what wonderful things we do in our youth, we don't know how or why! but as we grow older we become reflective, philosophical. Dramatic dialogue is very difficult. In a way it is like narrative description; it must *follow,* be coherent, and easy to read and listen to. For instance, I look out of this window. I see a sheet of water, a meadow, a stone wall, yellow flowers, tall trees and green lawns sweeping down to the river; the white clouds above, and so on. I can't jumble these all together; the sequence must be not only logical but easily apprehended by the reader. It's exceedingly hard to do. You can't jump about. —Now here is a good example of dramatic speech." He took up the text to read Ginger's long description of the race at the end of the first act. A sullen scowl spread over his features.

"What's this! Why, you've cut that speech!" He let the book slide from his hands.

I thought my reasons were good for cutting the speech, and I did my best to explain them. Moore reflected for a moment, and then:

"Well," he replied, "you are doubtless right about that. When the play was done in London the speech was spoiled because the actor rattled it off so fast nobody could understand a word." He then read it, slowly and with rhythmical emphasis, like a Dalcroze dancer performing an interpretative ballet. "Yes, you are right, I think: I am sure we couldn't find the actor for it, anyway."

It was nearly time for my train, and I got my hat and coat from where Moore had thrown them—a corner of the room. As we walked to the station we planned further modifications of the plot.

"I think," Moore concluded, "we agree on the essentials. You will re-write the scenes we have gone over together, and then send them to me. When I go back to London I'll add to the new act what I think is required, and then you can send your manuscript to America."

At the station Moore bought the latest papers from Paris, looking for news of the Carpentier fight.

"Listen to this," said he, spreading out the *Journal* over the bar where we had stopped for drinks: " 'It is estimated that each of the fighters will earn 4,500 francs a minute'. Well, we too may make that much if our play is ever produced!"

The train drew in, I hopped into my *troisième* with a bundle of manuscripts under my arm, as Moore stood with his umbrella in one hand and a crumpled newspaper in the other. He was gravely looking at me as the train pulled away, smoothed out his long moustache and with a quaint smile turned into the station.

.   .   .   .

Coming back now to the chronological narrative where I left it before telling of the collaboration on *Esther Waters*, I find myself at Foyot's, at seven-thirty, Tuesday evening, April 25.

Moore was waiting for me in the small lobby. He nodded the moment I appeared in the doorway, and without even greeting me, he scowled. "And where is Mrs. Clark, young man? Couldn't come? Or wouldn't come? Too bad, too bad: I had pictured her with us; we would have had a pleasant evening, the three of us, but I suppose she has her reasons. I hope they are good reasons. Well, let us be on our way, if you are ready."

And we walked in silence through the Rue de Condé to the Restaurant Voltaire. As we crossed the Place de l'Odéon I took his arm as I usually did, but Moore petulantly shook himself loose; this was a case of pure ill-temper, for he was really vexed. Outside a little shop in the Place a large dog jumped at him, and this was an added annoyance. "My God, now, what's this?" But the dog seemed friendly, so Moore stopped and stroked the animal.

Moore was impressed by the quiet austerity, the faded white tables and red plush of the Voltaire, and the little wine-server who walks on the balls of his feet. By the time he began discussing the menu with the waiter he had recovered his good nature, except for a moment when he learned that it would be necessary to send out for the *gros sel,* without which, he insisted, the fish "would not be edible."

Though I had no definite plan for writing a book, long or short, on the Paris of Balzac and Moore, I was playing with the notion of a few illustrated articles. I had brought with me several notes and my marked copies of the *Memoirs, Confessions,* and *Hail and Farewell.* During dinner Moore reminisced sporadically about his early days.

"Perren's, a famous old dance hall. That was in the Rue de Provence. It was there I met most of the famous cocottes of the day; I danced with them; I was a good dancer then. I am beginning to see here a wonderful article for you to write. Get photographs of these celebrated women; people are always interested in knowing what those beautiful whores looked like, and how they behaved. You might describe Hortense Schneider; oh, I could tell you a great deal about her that I have never used in any of my books."

"Ah, I recognize that photograph! Manet's studio, where he did his best work. Now a young ladies' drawing academy.

I visited the place a short time ago, and the concierge showed me the room I used to know so well."

We jumped from subject to subject as the pictures and notes were passed to him over the table.

"No, I remember very little about Bernard Lopez. A queer old fellow. He once collaborated with Gérard de Nerval, and *I* collaborated with *Lopez*. I must surely be the only man alive who ever collaborated with a man who collaborated with Nerval. Hanged himself in what street? Oh, Nerval, yes —the Rue de la Vieille Lanterne; doubtless he chose that street for its suggestive romantic name.—No, Augusta Holmés never interested me greatly. Tell your friend [Sidney Howard, who at that time was thinking of doing a play around her] to write about someone else. How can anyone write about Holmés? And a play, of all things! The only interesting thing I know about her is the report that she was the illegitimate daughter of Alfred de Vigny. Is there a play in that? No, no, tell your young friend to put it out of his mind.—But to return to your book, or your articles, you must not fail to write about Fontainebleau, or rather Avon, for it was there, at Dujardin's house, that I have done much of my writing. Dujardin is one of the most extraordinary men I have ever known. He's always digging in the strangest dark corners, of religion, or art, or anthropology, meeting the queerest people, getting involved in the maddest projects. One of his theories is that Jesus never existed: he was only an old Hebrew myth. Years ago he explained this to me and out of that germinal idea I began writing *The Brook Kerith*. Of course, I could scarcely write a whole book about someone who never lived, but the idea set me thinking; it would make a magnificent story, I said to myself. In order to approach my subject by way of a preliminary sketch I wrote *The Apostle*."

"And it was Dujardin, as I have written, who first introduced me to Wagner's music. We made many journeys to Bay-

reuth together. Yes, you must go to Le Val Changis and describe Dujardin and his house, and his beautiful lawns and
gardens. I have written many pages under his trees. I am going
there soon; he will invite you; *we* will invite you; in fact I am
now inviting you, so you must be sure to come."

" 'Lewis,' mentioned so often in *Hail and Farewell,* is of
course, a real person: Lewis Weldon Hawkins. He's dead now.
Another amazing character. He painted one successful picture
and his success so astonished and pleased him that he used to
go to the Salon every day and gaze at it."

"And here is your snapshot of what? A café? No, that is
not the 'certain ultimate café in the Latin Quarter' mentioned
in the *Memoirs.* That was the Café Medicis, where you had
tea the other day. I well remember the little girl I wrote about.
A pathetic girl—and a damn good story I did about her."

"It was Paul Aléxis who gave me the idea for my story of
The End of Marie Pellegrin, but Paul called her Lucie. He
based his version on hearsay, but I saw and knew her. The
end of my story is legend, where Marie steps out on the balcony to see the fireworks, and dies—but what a beautiful legend!" He paused a moment and pulled ruefully, reflectively,
at his long moustache. I had just read the Aléxis story and
Moore was curious to hear about it, since he had not seen it
since he was twenty-five. Which, he asked, was the better telling? No, honestly, he wanted to know. I said that Aléxis, writing evidently in the then new Zola tradition, had followed the
police report technique, and had given the tale little color or
variety. I was surprised, I said, that Moore, who himself had
learned the art of fiction from the Naturalists, had written little besides *A Mummer's Wife* in their style.

Moore mumbled something about fate and launched into
a bitter attack on Zola. "The man had no art. A clever man,
but too damned thorough. I remember one evening he came
to dinner at the home of La Valtesse, a famous cocotte—you
can see her portrait in the Luxembourg, painted by Gervex,

at one time her *amant de cœur*. Zola was collecting notes (My God, what masses of notes!), preparing to write *Nana;* he was in search of local color. I don't think he felt comfortable there, and clearly he had come for strictly scientific purposes; at any rate he scarcely looked at the woman, but asked at once to see her bed-room; and what do you think he wanted there? To measure it with a yardstick, get its exact dimensions! Good God! Art is a coquette, and Zola never suspected it; you must woo art. Zola was hardly what you would call coquettish. Why, Arnold Bennett's tart in *The Pretty Lady* is finer than anything Zola ever imagined; one of the finest prostitutes in all literature. But let us forget Zola and speak of La Valtesse, whom Zola treated so shabbily. I was at her salon one evening when Gervex and Manet were there. Manet's hair was red as hers—and mine, though hardly red, had a reddish tint. Wine was there in abundance and some of us were very silly. Gervex tried to make trouble by implicating Manet and me in a little plot to make La Valtesse jealous, but the woman understood Gervex too well to enter into the fun.—Gervex did good work when he was young, but he was ruined by his good looks: he fell in love with every pretty woman he met, and no woman could resist him. A handsome artist is at a great disadvantage, and Gervex went to hell. His Luxembourg portrait is very good, but all his later work is vile."

Though Moore had once dismissed Zola from the conversation he kept talking about him. "Zola and I," he said, "once wrote stories on the same subject. He called his *L'Inondation,* and mine was *A Flood.* One day Zola read in a newspaper about a family that had been drowned in a flood; only one member of it was saved, an old man. He said he would write that up as a *conte,* but I too liked the idea and said I would like to write a story based on the same plot. 'There is no reason why you should not write it, too,' he said. Mine was printed in *The Smart Set* about twenty-five years ago. No, it was never reprinted in book form, though I think it appeared on this side in *The Irish Review*. I never had the courage to read Zola's story. At first I was afraid it would be better than mine; maybe it is, but I am not so sure: Zola believed that because a thing was true it was necessarily a work of art."

"Take this Irishman Joyce, a sort of Zola gone to seed. Someone recently sent me a copy of *Ulysses*, which was published here a few weeks ago. I was told I must read it, but how can one plow through such stuff? I read a little here and there, but, Oh my God, how bored I got! Probably Joyce thinks that because he prints all the dirty little words he is a great novelist. You know, of course, he got his ideas from Dujardin? What do you think of *Ulysses*?" (I had no time to answer). "Joyce, Joyce, why he's nobody—from the Dublin docks: no family, no breeding. Someone else once sent me his *Portrait of the Artist as a Young Man,* a book entirely without style or distinction; why, I did the same thing, but much better, in *The Confessions of a Young Man*. Why attempt the same thing again unless you can turn out a better book?"

A pause: evidently Moore was reconsidering what he had said, and he so far qualified his remarks as to admit that Joyce's *Dubliners* had some good things in it. "But *Ulysses* is hopeless; it is absurd to imagine that any good end can be served by trying to record every single thought and sensation of any human being. That's not art, it's like trying to copy the London Directory. Do you know Joyce? He lives here in Paris, I understand; you pointed him out to me the other day? How does he manage to make a living? His books don't sell. Maybe he has money? You don't know? I'm curious. Ask someone that question."

"Did I tell you," he went on as though this had been part of the foregoing monologue, "that I have just been reading proofs of a French translation of the *Memoirs* that is to appear in the *Cahiers verts* series? The work was done by Daniel Halévy and someone else. It's not good. For some unknown reason they are leaving out *The Lovers of Orelay,* but I am not concerned over that: I am used to seeing my works ruined in translation. I called on the publisher the other day; he had never heard of me and I was embarrassed when I had to tell him that I enjoyed some little reputation as a writer in my own country. Just before I left his office the fellow patted me on the back and remarked that he imagined I must be a rather intelligent person."

"I have had no better luck with my books in Germany. *Esther Waters* was translated by a German literary hack, a man who had failed as an 'original' writer. He left out the baptism scene of Esther's child because, as he told me later, he considered it unnecessary. Why in God's name should a translator with no literary standing take it upon himself to do such things? There might be some justification if a man like Turgenev were doing the work. Why—! I venture to think that having written fifteen volumes of prose fiction I know nearly all there is to be known of that art. If I want to alter what I have written, that is my own affair. . . . Take Balzac—"

"So, here we are again, as usual, back to the subject of the immortal and ubiquitous Balzac. We can always find something to say about him, but as you know, for you too love Balzac, he is not really a 'good' writer. I have tried time and again to translate passages of his into good English."

"No man," I interjected, "is a hero to his translator."

"Why not put it this way? Every man is a hero to his valet, no man to his translator?"

"Do you prefer your epigram, Mr. Moore?"

"I—I don't know. Do you think yours better? Um—perhaps it is, my young friend, but let it go at that. And now that our dinner is ended, shall we walk back to my rooms at Foyot's?"

It was ten o'clock,—a hot evening with little air stirring. Arriving at Foyot's in five minutes, we walked up to Moore's small apartment. He strode over to a window and threw it way up, and motioned me to a chair in the small sitting-room while he retired for a moment into his bed-room. I thought he might be tired, so when he came back I suggested that I ought to be leaving.

"No, no, it takes us some time to get started, and you see I am in the mood to talk now. Unless, of course, Mrs. Clark is expecting you; you are both too nice to quarrel, but I daresay you don't quarrel anyway, so let me hear no more of your wishing to go."

"It wasn't that I wished—"

He waved me aside and sat in an uncomfortable arm-chair.

"We have talked enough about our play," he began, "so let us speak of other matters; the articles you are planning to write will prove a fruitful subject.—All is accident; nothing is foreseen in this life of ours. See what we have uncovered this evening (Keep away from that window—a *courant d'air,* you know! There!) possibly a valuable vein of subject matter. You were telling me of Hennique, and that set me to meditating on my early days in Paris. There are other men I knew well—writers, painters—who are still alive."

Yes, I should like to see Hennique, one of the last survivors of the Naturalist school of writers. "See him at once," Moore urged. "Don't lose a single day. Now if I were you this is what I would say to him: 'Monsieur Hennique, tell me exactly what are your impressions and memories of George Moore.' Never mind what he says; write it down; I will be interested to hear what he thought of me. Never mind if he says no more than that 'George Moore was a damned fool'; the important thing is to hear him say it. You tell me he lives just outside the Fortifications? Good, he has a garden, then; he must have a pretty garden where he walks in the morning and in the evening. Go and see him in his little garden, this old man who has now dropped so completely from the public view, almost indeed from the memory of man. He is surely a picturesque figure. Watch him, draw him out with your questions, and then describe him. Flatter him, if need be, at all events interest him and make him reveal himself to you. Tell him, if you like, of my efforts to get his beautiful play *La Mort du Duc d'Enghien* produced in England. Perhaps that will bring a flash into his eyes. Tell him, too, that I will gladly come out to see him if he would like that. But no matter how little he says to you, put it down, fix it in your memory, write it out, amplify his phrases and sentences. I would come into your paper only as a foil, an excuse, a shadow in the background."

Here Moore got up and began again describing vast circles in the air with his puffy but not ungraceful hands. He passed slowly between the arm-chair and the open window.

"On the other hand, Hennique may prove unexpectedly communicative; I can imagine him saying this to you, and in this fashion: 'Oui, je me souviens de ce jeune anglais—très gentil, ce Georges Moore. Il parlait français assez bien à cette époque-là. Il a collaboré avec Aléxis, mais pas avec moi.' Or else this, 'Oui, je me souviens: ce jeune homme était assez stupide.' If you know your business you will go out immediately and see him—in his pretty little garden outside the Fortifications. Go straight to his house."

The moment I could get a word in I promised to do so, and I went on to mention Henri Céard, another writer often mentioned in Moore's writings. I had recently read some of his stories.

"Yes, there was Céard, too, but he may be dead, I don't know. I was never very intimate with him, but he may help you. On the other hand I knew Aléxis well for many years. I know *he* is dead. No, I hardly think you will get much from Céard, even if he is alive: he had a sour disposition and I don't imagine old age has improved that. But Hennique is your best chance.—Then there's Forain—I'd almost forgotten him. See how you have roused these old memories! He knew me even before the others did. I saw him only a few years ago (we hadn't met for forty years), and he greeted me affectionately. See him, too, by all means. I am told he once made a sketch of me, and he might let you use it if he still has it. Gervex is another possibility, but I doubt if he will have much to communicate. But let me think more about this. You don't mind my planning your book for you? You see, it has grown to a full-sized volume now, and why not? I am always more interested in my friends' books than in my own. I see this book developing, branching out. Here you have Hennique and Forain already; possibly Gervex and Céard, and of course Moore; think the whole thing out, modify and amplify it, get the viewpoints of other men; and be sure to describe everyone, vividly, clearly. Ah, I am a poor hand at describing people."

"Is that false modesty? Surely your descriptions of people are what—"

"Don't try to flatter me!" This in a tone of irritation.

"But do you recall how you described Yeats in *Hail and Farewell?* 'He folded his wings like a pelican and dreamed of his disciples'."

"Did I write that?" he asked, smiling broadly. "I had forgotten. That is very good, but I can't do the kind of thing Balzac did; he pinned the character down, got him foursquare onto the page."

"I can't quite agree with that," I said. "I could quote other descriptions from your books, but I don't recall the exact words at the moment. Passages from *Esther Waters,* even from *The Confessions*—"

"Of course you can't, but you remember Père Grandet, and Père Goriot and the Curé de Tours? There you are. But to return to your own book: I wish I had time to write it myself. You will at least allow me to write the preface? I think I could do a very nice preface. It shall not be overloaded with 'hads,' I promise you, like that edition of *Memoirs of My Dead*

Life you brought with you. Promise me you will throw that away. Oh, dear, dear, how one's sins pursue one!"

"What is this other book you have? *Impressions and Opinions.*" He took up the volume and fingered the pages. "I want you to help me find a good title for the book that is to take its place in the new collected edition. I have thought of *Parleyings and Opinions.* How do you like that?"

I did not like it and I said so, adding that I thought he should avoid such colorless words as impressions and the like.

"That was Symons' fault. He named the book. How like Symons!"

I suggested other titles, and hit upon *Conversations* because of the colloquial style of most of the papers, and Moore seemed to like that. "I am going to introduce each of the rewritten articles with a few notes telling how it came to be written. Does that idea appeal to you? Most people seem to want that. Here now is the *Balzac* paper. It is not good. I am doing that over altogether; and the *Turgenieff,* too. This one on *Wellington* I'll let stand just about as it is. The *Zola* needs revision. I shall keep the articles on *Clairon, Mummer Worship,* and *Degas,* but the *Degas* is to go into the new *Modern Painting.* . . .

"The wonder of writing, and the art of it! There is something miraculous in it. I wrote all these essays when I was a very young man and knew nothing of the writer's craft. I think they were moulded by fate: one was good and another vile. After all, one is destined to write or not to write, as the case may be, and nothing—not even marriage, and no reflections on your charming wife!—is a legitimate excuse for not accepting and giving yourself up to your fate; or going out to meet it. If you are destined to do something you just do it and that is all. I had no idea, for example, that I could actually write *The Brook Kerith* or *Héloïse* until I had finished them. No, no one knows: you may write badly for a long time, and then suddenly turn out a masterpiece. One of the most extra-ordinary phenomena of modern literature, as mysterious as it is unquestioned, is the great number of writers who turn out one good book and no more. You could write a volume on that subject alone, yet come no closer to a true explanation."

"All of which, I take it, only goes to prove that you, Mr. Moore, are a born writer."

"Possibly, possibly, but you would think that by now I had gained some aptitude for the minor technicalities of my business, yet I find writing very hard. Why, even spelling troubles me. Look at this scenario of our play—see, I write *wrode* for *rode*. I shudder to think what anyone would say if he saw the first dictated drafts of *The Brook Kerith* and *Hé-loïse*. Inconceivably bad, clumsy, childish. I have to write and rewrite and revise before I can turn out anything half-way decent. Writing in longhand is hardest for me, but even dictating is difficult. You will notice how much better my typed letters are than those in longhand. Yet once in a while, as if by chance, I can dictate a whole paragraph that comes just right. A short time ago Heinemann asked me to try my hand (or rather my voice,) on a prospectus advertizing *In Single Strictness,* and I dictated it, and got it right the first time. Wait a minute."

He got up, brought a sheet of paper from the bureau and read as follows:

The five stories contained in this book may be considered as five chapters of one story. The first, *Wilfred Holmes,* tells of a man who is neither very stupid nor very clever and is remarkable for nothing but his complete inability to get a living. He has been brought up in a cage and, like a caged bird, has forgotten how to pick and perch. Sex barely touches him. In the second story we have two sisters—spinsters, one because of her devotion to her sister, the other from lack of sex impulse—and the characteristics of the two sisters are enshrined in a pathetic little story. *Hugh Monfert,* the third story and the longest, tells a tragic story and one which so far as we know has never been related before. The originality of this story in subject and treatment will take a very special place among Mr. Moore's narratives, and we think it will probably be given first place among the minor pieces—minor, that is, in length, although the story might be published separately, for in bulk it is not less than *The Lake.* The fourth story, *Henrietta Marr,* is remarkable for the unflinching severity with which the line of character is followed—a detestable girl, she yet retains our interest in that she is a human being. The last story, *Sarah Gwynn,* is a story of religious mysticism, and is likely to engage many sympathies and admirations. Many will think Mr. Moore never looked deeper into the heart. Like Esther Waters, Sarah is a servant, and the same strain of pity and reverence runs through this tale.

"That is just about how I dictated it, and by changing only a word here and there it was perfect. The Sarah Gwynn story, I think, is one of the best I ever wrote. It tells of a woman who"—and Moore, with his slow characteristic gestures of arm and head, told the whole story, and told it remarkably well.

"Yes, I often tell my stories far better than I write them, and I am afraid that *Sarah Gwynn* is not as well written as it should be."

In discussing *Henrietta Marr,* based on the story of *Mildred Lawson,* in *Celibates,* I asked whether Moore had read Huneker's essay on *Three Disagreeable Girls,* one of whom was Mildred. He had not, or he did not remember, but he spoke sympathetically of Huneker and his work.

"I never knew anyone with such literary facility; and since he spoke highly of my work why should I not feel well-disposed toward him? I am almost embarrassed when I recall all the pleasant things he said about me, but I was disappointed when I came to read his own novel, *Painted Veils.* After I had turned over the opening pages of that book I laid it aside and said to myself, 'He has done it! Done to perfection what I attempted in *Esther Waters,* but without success; he has done it ten times as well.' And then I read on and found the rest of the book trivial. He loses himself in details, and is always dropping the thread of his narrative. Very likely he had never trained himself to work his ideas out in orderly and consecutive fashion. I am afraid he had no narrative gift."

Now, in *Héloïse and Abélard,* he continued, there was striking evidence of his own gift for narrative. He was surprised by the reviews, but "disappointed because so few critics bothered to analyse the book carefully. It would have been easy to discuss the form, compare my treatment of it with others' treatment of similar themes, and so on, yet apparently no one thought of doing that. But I am not letting that bother me."

"Let me ask you—changing the subject—about this story of the outlaw mountaineer your wife told me the other day; I am writing it out and I shall need names of people and places."

"John McCusker was the outlaw's name," I said, "and the place of the story is the Potomac Valley near the town of Hancock in Maryland."

"McCusker—John McCusker is excellent. I shall use that. Potomac is good, too, but I hardly fancy Hancock. Oh, I do wish Mrs. Clark were here to suggest other names to me! She should have come with you tonight! Oh dear!—Maryland, you say?" and he pronounced it Mary-land. I corrected him, but he preferred the sound of *Mary*, with the long *Y*. "Blue Ridge Mountains' " appealed to him as perfect poetry and he repeated the words, making them sound like distant drums.

"Now tell me, since Mrs. Clark did not see fit to join us, what was the name of the woman who brought food and shoes to the outlaw? Was it Sarah?"

"It may have been, but I don't know."

"Sarah it shall be, then. Sarah it must surely have been." He made a mental note of this and sat down, pulling his moustache. "Motion pictures," he muttered, "movies, as you call them," and he wondered whether anything good would ever come of them; the thought occurred to him at the moment because this very morning two picture men had called to see him. He had consented to receive them because he was curious to know what they wanted. They asked him to write a short history of Ireland which could be used as the basis for a picture. "But why have you come to me?," he asked. They had been told that he was an Irishman as well as a man of some reputation in the world of letters. "I do know something about Ireland, and you must know that I am a literary artist; that is my profession; but let me tell you, your motion pictures are the negation of all art." One of the emissaries protested that the pictures were without question works of art, to which Moore answered that "art is a matter of personality, it presupposes a peculiar gift or talent—skill—a special kind of activity of the hand or the head. Besides, I know nothing whatsoever about the cinema; I have never even seen a motion picture. I therefore decline your offer."

He rose again and acted out the scene, dismissing the men with dignity and a theatrical flourish of the arm and a queer twisted sort of grin. Moore's face is by no means handsome. There is a trace in it of the old-time racing sport, and in his bearing something of the conventional ante-bellum Kentucky colonel. In repose the face is severe, with deep lines, but it is usually lighted with ironic humor and sympathy. The white moustache, with its sweeping curves, shows the front teeth when he smiles. His eyes are light blue and at times a little dull. The flesh of the face is full, pink as a baby's. The hair is thin and white and falls decoratively over his long forehead.

It was now after midnight, but Moore insisted on talking over the scenario of *Esther Waters* for at least another hour. I took advantage of a short pause and reached for my hat; at length Moore tacitly admitted that he was sleepy, and came down the hallway with me, murmuring that he was "sure" I was his "ideal collaborator," urged me not to work too hurriedly, and walked into the courtyard and out into the Rue de Tournon, now quiet and deserted. I had already started down the street when I heard him call out, "Don't make our play too damn mechanical, mind you!"

Two days later, about four in the afternoon, Muriel Harris Hueffer was having tea with Cecile and me in our room. After two loud knocks on the door, and without waiting for an invitation to enter, Moore walked in on us. He had climbed the five flights of stairs to our attic in some haste, and he threw himself unceremoniously into the chair nearest the door.

"My God, it's hot! You don't mind my bursting in on you this way, I hope? Oh—" (He had apparently just noticed Muriel, to whom I introduced him). "Oh, you are—yes. Mm— a pleasure." He then got up and, pointedly ignoring our guest, sat on the bed next to Cecile and began talking to her. Muriel, tactful as ever and very much amused, smiled at us and went out. Moore took no notice of her whatever, but as soon as the door closed he rather brutally gave us his unasked opinion of the first wife of Muriel's husband, Oliver Madox Hueffer. That delivered, he told us he had been working indoors all day and felt the need of fresh air and company. "I like this old room of yours, and I'm tempted to stay just where I am. If I knew you a little better I think I would stretch out on this bed and rest. However, we had all better go out now. Will you have tea with me? You must know of some pleasant quiet place nearby?" Before we could do more than murmur assent, Moore was sitting up very straight, looking more than ever like an exceedingly clean baby in his well pressed suit and neat purple shirt, and plunged into the middle of a discussion as though we had all been talking for the last hour. He was asking and answering questions about the building we lived in, the ancient Hotel de Ranes. He wanted to see the Myers' apartment downstairs, where Clairon and Lecouvreur had lived, and we agreed to show it to him on our way out. Cecile was now ready, and said so, but Moore turned to me, asking where the toilet was. I suddenly remembered Moore's lengthy commentary (in *Hail and Farewell*) on water-closets at some hotel in Bayreuth, but there was nothing for it but to point down the hall to an ancient door that led to what we and our friends called Rabelais' House, a "convenience" that had not been improved since the house was first built, in 1620.

"It's—it's rather primitive, Mr. Moore, but it's the best we have to offer." And he strode with superb dignity down the narrow corridor, while Cecile and I turned the other way and smiled. The old gentleman emerged a few moments later looking a trifle alarmed, and amused as well. "My God," he said in a soft and ingratiating tone, "it *is* primitive!"

We started to go down but Moore insisted that we should stand with him and talk about Clairon, so we stood chattering at the top of the stairs. "I imagine that she was not a very great actress: there's something about her name (though Clairon was not her *real* name) that suggests rhetoric and declamation. She must indeed have had a trumpet voice. You know, don't you, that Clairon was a very naughty girl!"

Yes, I had been reading the Goncourt book as well as the police reports made by order of Louis XV, in which Clairon was a prominent figure. Moore remembered the Goncourt book, but he thought his own review of it was better, "doubtless because I put a great deal of myself into it. Nevertheless, I paraphrased many passages, and that may account for the excellence of the paper. There are other books by the Goncourts' on Eighteenth Century actresses, aren't there? I think I saw *Sophie Arnould* on your table?"

I offered to lend him the volume, but he refused; then I promised to buy another and send it to him at Fontainebleau, but he told me I must not do that. "You are young, you must make a living; be careful, young man. Don't waste your money."

By now we had wandered back to our room and Moore picked up my copy of the French version of his Irish book, translated as *Terre d'Irlande*. As before, he expressed his loathing for it, saying that it consisted wholly of a series of hack articles he had written for the Paris *Figaro*.

"You have a delightful little room here," he went on and started to sit down, but thought better of it. "You must enjoy working here. My rooms at the hotel are impossible. I can do no work at all there. But come, we must be on our way."

Dick and Alice-Lee Myers were at home and we all went through their suite of old-world rooms, on the 3d floor below us. Moore was enchanted.

"I'm not interested in Lecouvreur, so do not, I beg you, speak of her; was she," he asked, turning to me as though I had known the lady personally, "was she a good actress? I am afraid not. No, Adrienne cannot have been a very good actress!"

"My dear young friends," this to the Myers', "if you should ever wish to rent your apartment I'll be glad to take it. I am a quiet and well-behaved old gentleman and will take the best care of your belongings. I can also furnish satisfactory references. Don't forget, now. Goodbye, goodbye." He strode out, Cecile and I close behind him.

We sat round a corner table at the Deux Magots for nearly two hours. Moore was hardly seated before he pulled a sheet of paper from his pocket, and a letter, and launched into an elaborate discourse on Hardy. He had recently amused himself by copying out in longhand a short passage from *The Return of the Native,* a striking bit of bad writing, and sent it to a friend (Hutchinson), a great Hardy enthusiast.

"Here is my friend's answer, and here is another passage from the same novel, which he claims is fine writing. Read it, read it aloud to me." I did, and either the passage was indeed very muddy or there was something in the evil twinkle of Moore's eye that made me think so; at any rate I had to admit that these paragraphs describing Egdon Heath were not in Hardy's best manner.

"Best manner? Good God, man, show me his best manner!" He chuckled, not, I think, so much because the writing was poor as that he had scored a point in an argument with his friend.

"If a novelist can't write his own language properly why speak of him as an artist at all?"

But Cecile and I tried to argue the point, and stuck to it that we both enjoyed Hardy—with some reservations.

" 'Reservations! Bloody nonsense! What do you see in him?"

We sensed something of the English countryside; atmosphere; a sense of character—

"Oh, yes, peasants dancing on the village green, and a whiff of wood smoke; farmers harvesting, a leafy lane or one of those stiff, wooden love scenes, so turgidly written. You admit that *The Mayor of Casterbridge* is mechanically contrived —you told me that the other day—but so is *Tess,* I tell you. It has no form at all. Yet people become ecstatic over Hardy, by God! and his precious art! True, they do the same with *Tom Jones,* another detestable book. I had to force myself to read that; and I expected something extraordinary. Fielding, too, has no sense of form, and no style. But Sterne on the other hand, is a master."

"Surely, Mr. Moore," I put in, "Sterne has less form than Fielding?"

"What? What?" But he said no more on that subject, preferring now to discuss our *Esther Waters* play. He was at this time putting the last touches on the scenario of the new act we had talked about, and this he planned to send me as soon as it came from the typist. "You can write that act very quickly; there is no more than a week's work to it. When you have finished it, send it to me at Dujardin's in Fontainebleau and I'll go over it there. That play in its new form ought to be a great success. I hope so. You will make lots of money out of it. We shall see. The important thing is to interest the actress, the right actress, who will play Esther. But we can discuss this at Fontainebleau."

"Now tell me about Hennique. Did you go out to see him, and did he have a pretty little garden?"

I had to admit that I wrote a letter instead, asking for an appointment. Moore's eyes fixed on me in a stare. He was annoyed, upset, perhaps even angry.

"You *wrote* to him? But didn't I tell you to go and see him?—Hm! What did he answer?"

"That he was leaving at once for Brussels, and that he had never known you very intimately. Would you care to see his letter?" Moore glanced at it. How much he read I don't know, but this is what Hennique had written:

". . . Have I met him four times in all my life? Not more. Once in the Rue de Douai, he was with Paul Aléxis; another time at Zola's; a third time at the home of the painter Edouard Manet; a fourth at Edmond de Goncourt's; and that is all. During one of his trips to Paris he came to see me but I believe I was laid up with the grippe, and to my great regret it was impossible for me to receive him. He wrote me, a long time since, from London, about one of my plays that was to be produced at some theater there, but I did not keep the letter . . ."

Moore gravely handed Hennique's letter back to me and said nothing more about it until later on. It was now nearly seven, and Moore seemed to have no intention of leaving, so Cecile asked him if he would care to dine with us at Michaud's. No, he had no engagement, and added ruefully that he felt lonesome. Each of us took one of his arms and we went down the rue Bonaparte to the rue Jacob, and then up to our room.

His mind had evidently been ruminating on the Hennique letter, for he gravely lectured me all over again because I had not followed his advice:

"I was sure of it! Something was bound to spoil our plan. I told you to go and see him and you did not. This is most vexing! Now tell me, what will you have to write about? Have you another article you can turn to? You cannot yet begin writing the third act of our play until you have received my outline. Dear me, you ought to have gone to *see* Hennique." And he stopped short in the middle of the street, turning gravely to look at a passing taxi. Then we walked on to the rue Visconti.

We climbed up the long stairs to our tiny room again, and on our way out to the street stopped in at Catherine Hopkins' place in the courtyard below. She had a studio in what was once the stable where Racine is said to have kept his coach and horses. A few weeks before Rosemary and Steve Benet had moved out and gone to England. There was something in Catherine's manner and looks, her militant youth and smiling happiness, that instantly captivated Moore. He had hardly shaken hands before he began his usual questions: "How old are you, my dear? Do you live here alone? Are you in love? What do you do to amuse yourself and how do you make a living? Ah, you draw? Let me see your work." By now we were seated in the main room of the little apartment, looking at the sketches that Catherine reluctantly took from her portfolios to show her guest.

"Yes, yes, indeed, a talent; perhaps not a great talent, still—Oh, I like that."

Catherine had another engagement that evening, but she promised to see Moore when he next came to Paris.

As we walked away down the rue Jacob, Moore asked a dozen questions about our "charming young friend." "A delightful girl, and how American! I am fated, it seems, to like Americans; and somehow they seem to like me, which is pleasant."

We crowded around one of the little marble tables at Michaud's tiny restaurant and ordered Moore's dinner for him; he would express no preferences, saying that we were sufficiently Parisian to choose wisely for him. Before I had finished ordering Moore was settled comfortably for a long talk and began, out of a clear sky, to tell us about Horace Live-right, who had come to see him in Ebury Street. He arrived at the house late one night, bringing with him a young novelist called—Lewis—er—Sinclair Lewis, and two women. Moore had been annoyed, especially when he was told by the maid that she had been unceremoniously thrust aside by the enter-prising publisher.

"I got rid of that rowdy party in a few minutes and then I sat down and wrote Liveright, telling him in no uncertain terms that I was ready to break off all relations with him. But he answered goodnaturedly that no one in America objected to receiving guests at all hours of the day or night, and that I ought not have been offended; he had the effrontery to say he would be quite willing to break off with *me*, 'were it not for my great admiration for your literary style.' Good God, he never read a line of anything I ever wrote!"

"I once told him a story that he wanted me to publish, but I am afraid I could not do that. Shall I tell it to you now? It's a little scandalous. You wouldn't be bored? Let me see:

"Watts-Dunton lay ill in bed, at the point of death. Never-theless, he had consented to see Wise, the book and autograph dealer who had come to buy some Swinburne manuscripts. The talk drifted from matters of business to Swinburne's poems, and Watts-Dunton, though physically weak, recited one of the more sensuous Greek poems; it was a description of some naked goddess. From poetry the conversation turned to naked women, and Watts-Dunton, the ass, remarked that he had never seen one. Wise was astonished, the more so when he remembered that Watts-Dunton had once been married.

" 'Ah,' the sick man commented, 'that was a strictly pla-tonic marriage. Do you not think it shameful and regrettable that I should leave this life without having at least looked at this marvel which is the inspiration of poets and the supreme experience—er—that is—'

"Wise could scarcely believe his ears, but when he was convinced his friend was telling the truth he suggested that there might still be time. Watts-Dunton, a little feverishly, I imagine, asked what he meant by that? Miss ——, who was a sort of assistant or secretary in the house, was an attractive woman and she might, under these unusual circumstances, consent to oblige him. So then and there, Miss —— was summoned and the two men explained that they wished her to undress and stand for a moment before Watts-Dunton.

"She was a modest young lady, yet she was inordinately proud of her beauty, and since she had been told by the doctor that Watts-Dunton had not long to live, she consented, but— she insisted that Wise step outside into the hallway. In a moment, behold, she stands naked as Venus rising from the waves, while the poet, propped up on his pillow, contemplates her with rapture. With a deep sigh he thanks the lady, who hurriedly dresses, and sinks back exhausted.

"The next day he is not so well, and again he begs the lady to repeat her favor, and she complies, adding a touch of coquetry by some slight turn of the body, and again Watts-Dunton sinks back exhausted and happy. And on the third day the performance is once more repeated. On this occasion Watts-Dunton is so transported that he extends his arms toward the lovely vision and the next moment falls back on the bed, breathing his last sigh."

"Do you think," he asked us, "I would dare publish that story? I might be sued for libel; but it really ought to be published. It belongs properly in *Avowals;* ah, that would then be a book for the ages! But I don't know—. The best part of it is that I would put the tale into the mouth of Gosse."

"You mean, make it Gosse's story? What would he say to that?"

"He would say nothing until he saw it in print, and then he would never think of scolding; he is too fond of me. But I am not worrying about Gosse; what of the lady?"

"Need you use her name?" Cecile asked. "You know, she might be flattered by your description of her charms?"

"Very likely she would, my dear, and sue me for two

thousand pounds. That would not be so pleasant. Possibly I might allow Liveright to print it and risk being sued. Or I might leave it in the form in which I first wrote it, like one of the *Contes drolatiques;* perhaps that would not be libelous? What do you think?"

We didn't think, but that meant nothing to Moore; he only wanted to tell the story.

"Did Gosse really tell you the story?" I asked, though I knew it was Moore's own invention.

"No, but he might have."

James Joyce came into the restaurant at this point, with two women (his wife and daughter?), and sat down opposite us. Joyce looked at Moore out of his one good eye, the other being covered with a black patch, and Moore stared back at him. It was embarrassing for us to hear Moore inquire in a stage whisper whether that fellow was Joyce? He said nothing more except to inquire again how Joyce made his living. We could not say.

By now Moore was tired and spoke only in short sentences, jumping from subject to subject. Dujardin, he remarked, was once again in financial difficulties and Moore had authorised him to sell any of the letters he had written him, but admonished him to correct the grammar and spelling (most of these letters were written in Moore's very faulty French), whereupon Dujardin had answered, "What the hell's that to you?" Moore was furious, but I sided with Dujardin, saying that these letters, some of which I had seen, were not intended as literature, that they were personal and intimate revelations of the writer. Moore looked at me as though he had not understood, and only shrugged his shoulders.

On the way back to Foyot's he wondered again how Joyce made his living: "I never made any money out of my books, not a great deal. Pocket-money, yes, but little more."

"I want to tell you, now that we are about to say Good Night, what great pleasure you have both given me. And you have given me help, besides. For example, though I have known for a long time that the play *Esther Waters* needed revising, I daresay I should never have got round to doing the work except for your urging. Believe me, this is not flattery; I am a poor hand at flattery.—Did I ever tell you about Berenson?"

"The art critic? No, I think not."

"This will take only a minute, and I must not keep you. Here we are at Foyot's already. Well, one day Berenson wanted to draw me out—pump me, rather, on some matter, I forget what, so he invited me to what I supposed would be a dinner. I enjoy good food and I want enough of it, but he served tiny coquilles of chicken, a little cheese and coffee. I was disgusted—I assure you I was in an evil humor. We got up from table and went into the library where Berenson offered me a chair and began asking questions. He handed me a cigar but, by God, I was afraid it would make me sick, so I told him bluntly I was not in the habit of smoking before dinner. I got up, walked out of the house, and went to a restaurant.—But enough of Berenson.

"I leave shortly for Fontainebleau, where I look forward to the pleasure of seeing you both. Good night." With a quick nod of the head, he turned squarely about, waved his hand and without looking at us again, marched off.

Moore made his visit to Dujardin at Avon, and on May 2 he acknowledged the receipt of the Sophie Arnould book I sent him. "The weather is detestable," he went on, "and I am discouraged, but I must write the preface. I look forward to seeing you and Mrs. Clark on my return. I hope she will be able to come to dinner this time." On the 4th came another note, expressing surprise at the speed with which I had worked over my version of *Esther Waters*. He was "in the middle of the preface for my collected works and hope to finish it this week." Nearly a week later I received the letter I have already mentioned earlier in these pages.

I arrived at the Avon station (Fontainebleau) on Friday morning May 12. My day there, so far as it was devoted to work on the play, I have recorded in the section where I discuss that entire matter. But to go back now and gather up the thread of my narrative, as Moore would phrase it, I shall fill in the picture with those details of the day at Avon which I left out when I was discussing the play.

In spite of the pouring rain, Moore began talking the moment I stepped out of the train, holding his umbrella over me for a few moments and then forgetting to hold it over either of us, as we made our way slowly through the muddy winding streets.

What did I think of the Genoa Conference? What can be done about the financial crisis in America? "If America has all the gold," he inquired, "why doesn't she re-distribute it and start trade going again?" The whole thing looked damn silly to him, but neither of us could suggest a solution, and I at any rate was interested in other things.

Turning into a quiet street, with high stone and plaster walls on either side, we came shortly to an old door sunk deep in a crumbling wall. This was the entrance to Dujardin's house, Le Val Changis. There is a long twisting walk of ancient brick leading from the street down a pathway sheltered by huge aged trees, to the house itself. The estate extends way down to the river, a quarter of a mile away. A perfect 17th Century estate, with a magnificent park; there was something here that reminded me of the Petit Trianon and something of the Duchesse de Montmorency's little house at Chantilly. We walked briskly down the damp pathway, under low-swinging boughs, right up to the porch of the house, and in through the tall open windows of the library.

Dujardin does a good deal of entertaining, and the first people we met were two young French journalists, to whom

Moore introduced me with the utmost casualness. Then Dujardin joined us. An altogether charming fellow, tall, lithe, youthful in speech and manner; white hair, wonderful blue eyes, thick but mobile and expressive lips. Decidedly a genial personality. He was friendly and cordial and asked me to sit down, but Moore was surly, and dragged me by the arm upstairs to talk about the play.

As I have already told, Moore resented Dujardin's interrupting us for luncheon, but at table he unbent as soon as the conversation began to interest him. But most of the time I am convinced he resented the presence, possibly the existence, of the young Swiss woman who joined us at table, an agreeable girl who has been living for the past few years with Dujardin.

We four men talked constantly at luncheon, jumping from topic to topic: Proust's latest book; Tolstoy; Romain Rolland; the technique of novel-writing; what not. We all spoke French and it seemed to me that Moore was more fluent in this company than he had been before—when he got a chance, that is, to put in a few words.

From the occasional remarks of Moore, I recollect the following:

He had read some of Proust; thought him clever but without a sense of artistic selection. "Doubtless my judgment is at fault, or my taste, for I am out of sympathy with his generation; and I imagine that *I* cannot as an artist appeal to the intellectual sympathies of the present generation. When I wrote my essays on the Impressionist Painters for a London paper I was of my day; I was the more or less accredited representative of what was then new; I had something to communicate, and the public I addressed was interested."

"Mais, mon ami," Dujardin put in, "if you wrote articles in the papers today about our modern art you would also interest your readers. Your viewpoint would be stimulating."

"Possibly, possibly," mused Moore, "yet I imagine that I would present only the spectacle of an outmoded elderly gentleman speaking my mind; I should in no sense represent my generation, nor could I express the sentiments and aspirations of the youth of today."

One of the newspapermen was telling us about a young novelist who was at work on a twelve-volume novel, and from that the conversation turned to *Jean-Christophe*. Moore asked me how long the Rolland book was, and I said I thought it might run to seven hundred thousand words.

"As long," he said, "as *War and Peace*. I read the first four volumes of Rolland's book and thought them very good, but I was not moved to read more: you just cannot write ten volumes about one man, about a musician who fails in life."

I here put in my word: "But should we not consider *Jean-Christophe* a vast description of the life of an epoch rather than just a novel *about* a man?"

"Quite right," said Dujardin. "It really makes no difference whether you call the book a novel or a history or what ever; if it is good in itself what more can we ask?"

"Perhaps," said Moore, "but after all, the length of a work must be determined by the interest and importance of its subject. *War and Peace* is a long book because war and peace are long things; the *Iliad* and the *Odyssey* are precisely the right length. In any event I prefer Homer to Rolland, because the Greek poet does not moralize. He paints."

This led to the question of writing in feuilleton form, and Dujardin asked Moore whether he had ever published anything serially.

"Yes, *Spring Days*. A good book, but the public didn't care for it. I shall include it in my collected works." He turned to me and suggested, in English, that we make our escape upstairs the moment we were through eating.

We went into the library for coffee, but remained only a few minutes, during which the talk centered upon Claudel, a writer whose works Moore had not read.

He asked me about the Claudel plays, but when I mentioned the title *L'Annonce faite à Marie,* he declared he would not read that one, at least!

"Oh, it's not about the Virgin? Then I promise to read it, provided, of course, you are right, and the Virgin is not a character on the stage. But now let us go to my room. Dujardin will have to do without our company for the rest of the afternoon." And up we went.

.   .   .   .   .

Ten days after my sojourn at Avon I wrote Moore asking him to return the third act of *Esther Waters,* since I had some corrections to make in the script. Three days later (May 23) Moore came to our room in the Rue Visconti. It was stifling hot and for the first time he looked just a little untidy: his usually sleek hair and moustache were ruffled and his gaudy tie askew. With a short word of greeting he walked into the room and threw himself down on the bed with a sigh. He then pulled the script of the third act out of his pocket and held it toward me.

"Here is the act you asked for. I've come to Paris to see my banker, and here I am. I came here to your room at once."

Cecile and I had not yet lunched and we suggested going out, but Moore had already eaten and he preferred to rest and talk. He was anxious to give us news about *The Coming of Gabrielle,* which some new manager wanted to produce in London for a few special performances in the autumn. "These people," he said, "are planning to produce several plays, including some of Granville Barker's. I wish they would do mine first, because people won't pay money to see Barker's. The fellow has no talent, I say. He once gave me a play of his to read, all about a cabinet minister who got a woman into trouble. The damn thing's full of politics and moralizing, and so dreadfully dull! Too bad, because Barker's a bright and charming fellow—personally. Do you know his new book on the theater? Pretentious, serious, *educational,* by God! I was asked to review it for the *Times,* but I would not do it. He prattles about educating the public by means of the theater. What the hell does he want to do that for?—And now, enough of this. Tell me, how much do you think the new manager should give me on signing the contract?"

Now that he was more comfortable (though he refused to take off his coat, as I had done), and I had answered his question, he got up and walked around the room, taking books from the shelf, asking more questions, and making himself entirely at home. I showed him the copy of his early play, *Martin Luther,* which I had got indirectly through the heirs of Lizzie Gardiner. He looked at his own inscription on the fly-leaf and began reading passages from the text.

"Not much as literature, I must confess, but there's a swing to this verse that's not half bad. The wonderful thing is that I was able to do it at all. I *did* write the whole bloody thing straight through, didn't I?"

It now occurred to Moore that perhaps we might be hungry, so he said he would go with us while we ate. We went to Michaud's and ate a light luncheon while Moore sipped iced coffee.

Though he and I had agreed to do our respective jobs on the re-writing of *Esther Waters* without discussing the matter until we were through, Moore said he couldn't resist the temptation to ask Cecile what she thought of his suggestions to me on my part of the rewriting. Cecile agreed with me but we both knew it would be useless to argue it out on this stifling day, so Cecile tactfully hinted that she thought a little more should be shown of the meeting between Esther and Mrs. Barfield in the new third act. Yes, not a bad idea, Moore agreed, but he saw no way of doing this except at the risk of spoiling the rest of the act.

I changed the subject by asking Moore what he intended to do with his novel *Vain Fortune?* Reprint it in the collected works? Revise or rewrite it? He wanted to revise it, but he could not get hold of the American (Scribner), edition, which in his opinion was the most satisfactory. I promised to get a copy for him.

"I know better now what to do with the man in that book. When I wrote the story I tried to explain him; now I realize that all I need to do is *show* him. How explain the inexplicable? Think of Becque, now, who spent years of his life talking about some masterpiece he was going to write; explaining it to his friends but never finishing it; and there's Dukas, the composer, eternally explaining, but doing nothing. It's the same with characters in a novel: you study a man for a whole lifetime and in the end you know nothing about him but what you can describe."

Moore here repeated what he had told us before, that he was not good at describing people. Not long since, five of his artist friends, Sickert, Steer, Tonks, Harrison, and another (McColl?), jokingly complained to him at a party that they had not been fully described in any of Moore's books.

"In my new preface to the collected works, after I finish laying out Hardy, I introduce these five. Little vignettes, you know, but I think I have done them extraordinarily well. I invent a characteristic anecdote for Harrison, who is an exquisite, a sensitive fellow. I have him go to Hampton Court where he complains that the colors of the flowers hurt him. I develop that idea at some length. Oh, the mere facts of the matter are not true, of course, but they might have been.—And then Sickert. A handsome man; no woman could resist him: his life has been a long series of women. At last, oh my God! he fell in love with the plainest-looking woman you ever saw, and married her! She died not long ago and the poor fellow was all broken up—couldn't paint for a year. Do you think he would like me to tell that in my book? Naturally, I would omit mentioning his wife's homeliness or—perhaps not—I don't know. About the other sketches I shan't bore you by telling them; you may read them when the preface is published."

I had just asked a question about *Evelyn Innes,* but Moore ignored this and told us about the woman on whom the character was based. I believe he said it was the present Lady ———. Before he began the book he had made up his mind that he wanted to write about convent life, but his intention was known to only a few persons. He got a letter from this woman saying that she had lived for a time in a convent and would be pleased to give him facts and background, provided it was not his intention to write in a disrespectful or scandalous fashion.

"Well," Moore said, "we met and we fell in love. From time to time the affair promised a happy termination but invariably, at the psychological moment, she had terrific qualms of conscience. At one time during our friendship she was in a bad state, telling me that while she had always wanted to have lovers her religion invariably stood in the way. It was all the fault of those damned priests! They put the fear of hellfire into her. I waited patiently for her during three years and then we met, accidentally, in Rouen, and she told me she would be mine. But I wasn't interested in her any longer, I just didn't want her. That was a blow. However, since then we have become good friends, the best friends in the world. I admire and respect her. She went into politics and now she seems happy, quite happy, I believe."

I am afraid I have confused this story in the telling, but Moore's narrative was rather vague. For one thing it seems to belie what he said a few days later to Catherine Hopkins, but, I leave this as it stands, adding only that Moore told us he had written about this woman and described the meeting at Rouen in one of his books, either *Avowals* or the *Memoirs.*

As we were speaking of the expected production of *The Coming of Gabrielle* Moore was reminded of the Independent Theatre in the early nineties. Grein, he admitted, had something to do with the new venture. Shortly after the founding of the Independent in 1891 Grein had come to Moore and asked him to start rehearsing a certain play, probably *Ghosts*.

Since Moore was one of the directors he did as he was told, rehearsed the play, and made a good job of it, so he says. But on the first night "Grein appeared before the curtain and without even mentioning me, he took all the credit for the production, and the whole undertaking as well. That was the end of my association with Grein. Since then he has often tried to see me again, but when I quarrel it is for *always*. I was through with him. Grein speaks and writes English with a thick Dutch accent."

It was now half-past two and Moore would have to go at once to his bank. We all got into a taxi, drove to the Place Vendôme and left him for a short while. Catherine Hopkins had come with us, having joined us at Michaud's. Then we all drove back in an open cab and in spite of the excessive heat, Moore talked all the while, addressing most of his remarks to Catherine. During the fifteen minutes of our drive he laid down the law again on the subject of popular education, the proper way to translate French into English, and the grammatical faults of Conrad and Hardy. Perhaps he was aware that generalizations weren't quite the thing for a hot May afternoon in Paris, for he next turned his attention to personal matters.

"What have you been doing since I saw you last, Miss Hopkins? Art? No? Oh, oh, then you must be in love?"

"Is that the only other alternative?"

"The word alternative, my dear young lady, leaves no room for more than one other, does it?"

"I'm sure I don't know; that is your business as a master of English."

The taxi driver thought it would be a good idea to know exactly where we wanted to go, so Catherine told him to leave us at 21 Rue Visconti. Would Mr. Moore have tea with us in her studio? He certainly would, but not today. Why make tea in this suffocating heat? Really, that would be senseless.

Would we not all be his guests at the Deux Magots? So to the Deux Magots we went, and sat sipping orangeades for two hours.

Moore continued to address himself to Catherine, who had just been buying her summer clothes. She had ordered what she called a "loud dress." Moore had never heard the expression before, and on being told its precise meaning he smiled and said, "I must remember that: a magnificent expression. 'Loud'."

Catherine wanted to know what Moore thought of Forain. She was trying to make up her mind to spend some of her hard-earned money on a Forain drawing. But Moore doesn't care much for Forain. "He uses the same lines every other draftsman uses. Compare him, for example, with Monnier— ah, there was a true artist; or Daumier. But no, my dear, not Forain." Catherine was unconvinced.

Had we seen Freeman's book on Moore? Moore has been reading it lately and often speaks of it. Sometimes he likes it and sometimes he finds it full of faults. He was today especially disdainful of the critic for taking him (Moore) to task for using "conventional words." "Why, everything in art is conventional; it depends on what conventions you choose to adopt. The use of unconventional expressions is itself a convention."

Once again we spoke of *Ulysses,* and Moore wanted Catherine's opinion. Catherine saw nothing in it, and said so.

"Oh, but that's abuse. There is no point in reading a book just to abuse it. I expect you to tell me what the book is, what the author has tried to do, and then criticize him if he has failed to accomplish his aim. There is no point in abuse. I am reminded of an Irishman I once knew, who read naughty books and complained of their naughtiness. I told him not to read them unless he got pleasure from them. Catulle Mendès was like that, too. He would introduce characters into his books, make them do things he disapproved of, and then blame them for their behavior. That was funny!"

Though it was nearly time to eat again none of us thought of food, and when Catherine again suggested her studio, Moore at once accepted the invitation.

The first thing he noticed on entering were the photos of the famous Holbein drawings of English historical figures. He stood rigid before the first of these, like a German officer at attention, stooped to examine a delicate line, then turned round to us and with a slow flourish of the arm announced, "There, that was something worth doing. To have achieved such perfection was worth any sacrifice. You, Miss Hopkins, an artist, will surely agree with me?"

But Catherine, though she may have agreed, wanted to prolong the argument and ventured to suggest that there might be something in life better and more important even than art.

"Oh, dear, dear, and what might that be?"

"Having children, for instance."

"Dear, dear! And I was just telling our friend Clark here on the way from the café that if I were a young man again you are just the sort of girl I could fall in love with! I take that back. You disappoint me. Children? Babies! Other people, the masses, can have children, more than enough to keep up the world's supply; but you can draw, my dear! Don't you really believe that one of these Holbein drawings is worth more than a whole litter of babies? Birth may be such a terrible thing, you know. Your baby might turn out to be a murderer!"

"I don't think this can be argued about, Mr. Moore. While my baby might turn out to be a murderer, it might also turn out to be another George Moore."

"Ah, don't imagine, young lady, you can win this argument by flattering me. But no matter. I want you to tell me, speaking of babies, if that baby carriage I saw outside your door belongs to you? Explain that if you can!" The carriage, he was told, belonged to the concierge, but Moore was already imagining a story about "a charming young girl who has a career but believes that a baby is more important. She tries to succeed in her art but falls in love and becomes a mother. Yes, I may write that story. You have given me an idea, my dear, a very good idea."

Quick preparations were made for tea, but the talk went on: Rodin was dismissed as "an imitation Italian Renaissance sculptor and probably a Jew; no Jew was ever a great artist . . . Cats are wonderful and lovable animals; civilization is going to the dogs because great pictures are reproduced in the form of cheap photographs.

"There are too many people in the world," Moore mused. "The struggle for existence is a result of that, and wholesale ugliness is manufactured to satisfy the masses. Instead of graceful prancing horses we have millions of hideous iron machines. Human beings swarm about us and crowd out so much that is beautiful."

"During the war a building near Chelsea Hospital was struck by a bomb and three people were killed. A friend was telling me about this and spoke of it as a terrible tragedy. 'Thank God,' I said, 'the Hospital was not harmed!' 'But' said my friend, 'think of the poor patients who might have suffered.' 'My dear friend,' I replied, 'I am not thinking of the patients, but of Christopher Wren's masterpiece. That could not be replaced.' 'You are cruel,' he said, 'you forget the human lives; they cannot be replaced.' I told him that was utter nonsense, that nothing was easier than to replace human lives. All you need is a healthy young farmer and a servant girl. Absurd, this prattle about the sacredness of human life!"

Moore was in such good spirits that Catherine ventured to ask if he would mind if she tried to make a sketch of him. Not in the least; he would take an easy position in that armchair. She worked for ten minutes, Moore chatting on and glancing at the sketch only when Catherine offered to show it to him. It was not very good, they agreed, so Moore offered to come again next Sunday afternoon.

As he was sitting for his portrait he told us more about "that extraordinary Dujardin."

"Many years ago he saw the photograph of a woman in some opera program, perhaps it was a Wagnerian magazine— a German woman, daughter of a kapellmeister who lived in Dresden. He swore she was the only woman he could ever love. Somehow he learned her name and address, wrote her a letter and told her how he felt about her. She answered and asked him how it was possible for him to be attracted by a woman who so obviously lacked physical beauty. Since she did not positively forbid him to come to see her the crazy fellow bought himself five-and-twenty fancy waistcoats, took the first train for Dresden and went to see her. Dujardin thought he was mad about her, but it seems she did not entirely reciprocate his passion; she married a parson shortly afterward. I was with Dujardin when the news came and I just prevented him from killing himself; as a matter of fact, I snatched the revolver from his hands. But instead of committing suicide he wrote three plays about his woman. The first of them was *Antonia.* Oh, my, a terrible mess of a play! Dujardin acted in that, and I believe in the other two as well. The last part of the trilogy was so absurd that the people who had come, nearly all of them Dujardin's friends, began to shriek with laughter. Dujardin stepped from behind the curtain and scolded the audience; since they were his guests, he told them they must be courteous enough to refrain from laughter; if they didn't like the play, they were at liberty to go home."

Max Beerbohm was our next topic of conversation.

Moore doesn't care for the Beerbohm cartoons. "They aren't drawings at all; the wit, when there is any, lies in the words that explain the caricature. He's no draftsman, but as a writer he has a certain small gift for pretty phrases."

He cares little for Galsworthy, "The novels are pale and the plays are paler. No, I shan't read *The Dark Flower,* which you tell me you like: my secretary read it and she tells me it is a poor thing. There's no blood in Galsworthy. Why, when he was divorced he tactfully allowed his wife to get the necessary evidence against him: to do this he was forced to go to the home

of some woman, hang up his hat and coat in the hallway, and—
that was all. Wasn't that sweet of him? Oh, no, no hint of im-
propriety! Why on earth couldn't he have made use of his
chance?"

There was no malice in this, harsh as the words sounded.
Moore was just enjoying the humor of the situation he had imagined. He lapsed into silence, and then slowly reaching for
his felt hat, stood upright, squared his shoulders, reminded
me of our meeting next Sunday, and announced that he was
going to return to Dujardin's, "in spite of that damn crying
baby!"

Before Moore left Paris again for Fontainebleau he had
asked me to reserve a room for him at Foyot's; he intended to
return to Paris on Saturday night. I made the reservation and
wrote him a letter of notification.

On my way back from the Luxembourg Gardens late Saturday afternoon I passed by Foyot's. Standing in the doorway
were Moore and Catherine. I greeted them and started on my
way, but Catherine insisted that I should join them. I learned
that Moore had taken a violent dislike to Le Val Changis, Dujardin, the Swiss girl and her "insufferable" baby, and had left
before he planned to. He had gone straight to the rue Visconti, found that Cecile and I were out, called on Catherine
and asked her to dine with him.

I hesitated again, afraid that Moore wanted to be alone
with Catherine, but she again insisted that I should come with
them to the Voltaire, and though Moore was a little put out he
was anxious to tell me all about his recent griefs. He had quar-
reled with his host and ordered Dujardin to summon a cab
to call for his trunk, but it had not come and the trunk was
taken to the station on a wheelbarrow by a servant, Moore
walking by his side, trying to keep the trunk from falling into
the muddy street. He had reached Paris last midnight, and

gone to Foyot's. No room for him there, which annnoyed him, and on being told that the room I had reserved for him was for Saturday, he was furious. There was his trunk in the courtyard of the hotel, the taxi was gone and not another in sight.

"I had no money with me, and there wasn't a room for me at the hotel, and evidently no chance of going elsewhere; and I certainly didn't like to ask the man at the desk to lend me money. The porter went out to look for a cab but came back half an hour later, unsuccessful. At last they told me I might sleep on one of these damn little wooden benches in the courtyard, so I curled up and managed to get some rest. It wasn't until six in the morning that they found a bed for me; probably they turned one of the servants out of his room. My God, how I slept! I didn't wake up till one in the afternoon. I can still feel those hard slats on the bench where they dug into my hind end! Oh, I forgot to tell you about my heel!" And he pointed to the felt slippers he was wearing.

"I couldn't put on one shoe. That heel got infected at Avon—it must have been a mosquito bite." He was the picture of limping misery. But after we had ordered food at the Voltaire his good spirits returned, and while he complained at great length about Dujardin, there was little bitterness left in him.

"But I have made my last visit to Le Val Changis. Dujardin is always in trouble of some sort, people buzzing about him constantly, dull, disagreeable men and women. He seems to go out of his way to meet the troublesome things, while I spend my life trying to avoid them. I declare I don't think he can be happy unless he's in hot water. If it's not money, it's women; just now, it's money *and* a woman. The woman there is eating her heart out for furs and diamonds and he's fool enough to try to give them to her. I marvel how he can stand the baby! When I left him the other day I told him he would never change; he would find himself on his dying day right in the midst of the usual mess and troubles."

Even now, after the "quarrel," Moore found himself involved in one of these troubles, and he told of a play written
by one of Dujardin's former mistresses, an ex-ballet dancer at
the Opera. "An impossible woman, but I promised I would go
to see her play. It is to be performed tomorrow night, and
you two and Mrs. Clark must come with me; not otherwise
shall I be able to survive the ordeal. The play is a dramatization of some incident in her life. She and Dujardin went
over the manuscript together some weeks ago, and the two
of them wept over it! Good God, what a man! She wrote a
book of reminiscences and one anecdote was six hundred
pages long; now, what are we to expect of her play? She once
asked me what I thought of her book and I told her that if she
had stopped posing as a vestal virgin among all the wicked
little dancers, admitting that she too was only a whore, neither
better nor worse than the rest, her book might have some
touch of freshness and originality. I don't know and I don't
care what she thought of my remarks. She asked for the truth
and the truth is what I gave her."

Moore was pleased as a child to learn that Catherine had
read his story *Wilfrid Holmes,* which appeared recently in the
London Mercury. "Oh, I *am* glad you liked my story. You think
the character is successfully drawn?" And he told how he had
followed with deep interest a long correspondence in some
London newspaper on the question of bird songs. He had used
in his story many of the facts discussed in the controversy, and
had himself listened to blackbirds, believing that some birds
are capable of making a complete melody. When he was in
quest of a commonplace musical theme to show what his composer had written he was puzzled to know where to find it, until on returning from Fontainebleau last year he heard a party
of people in the train singing the melody he has noted on the
last pages of *Wilfrid Holmes.* He hummed it to us.

Speaking of this story, which is to be a part of the book
In Single Strictness, he mentioned another tale, *Henrietta*

Marr, that is also to go into that collection. Its basis is the earlier story, *Mildred Lawson,* and *Elles et lui,* which is in the revised version of *Memoirs of My Dead Life.* The same woman served as model for all these stories.

"I don't see why I shouldn't tell you all about her. She was an American, P——, who wrote under the name of John Oliver Hobbs. I have known many women and loved many. Most women are charming and delightful but the only positively disagreeable woman I ever knew was this one. She was thoroughly bad, she was horrible. The daughter of a wealthy American, a manufacturer of patent medicines—liver pills. She had written to me—this was many years ago—sending me one of her novels, asking if I thought it could be made into a play. I answered briefly, saying I thought it a very pretty book but it did not seem necessary or wise to make a play of it. So the matter was dropped until some time later Arthur Symons told me that 'John Oliver Hobbs' was not a man, but a most attractive woman. That—was a different matter! I saw her some days afterward at the theater and thought she was amazingly beautiful. Well, one thing led to another, and I fell in love with her. I did. I'd like to deny it, but I cannot. We saw each other nearly every day for six months, and there were many 'passages' between us. We were very intimate but she would never allow me actually to become her lover and I was frantic. Then she went after another man, Lord —— —and one day when we were out walking in the woods she told me she didn't want to see me any more. I was dumbfounded, heart-broken, miserable. I looked her straight in the eyes and saw she was laughing at me, making sport of my miserable plight. An inexplicable woman. I was blind with rage, and I deliberately kicked her, kicked her squarely in the bottom. Then I turned and walked away.—That very incident is used, after a fashion, in *Henrietta Marr.* I went to France and Germany soon after, and tried to forget her. I fell in love again, —with another woman. Some years afterward she wrote me a letter and said she wanted to see me, but I told her that there would be no point in that. She insisted, and I was fool enough to go to her, and the whole damn miserable business began all over again. It seems that the Lord's wife was an invalid and P—— wanted the lady to die, so that he might marry *her*, but she refused to die. That was why P—— came back to me. Then she wanted to write a play for Forbes-Robertson and Ellen Terry, and asked me to suggest a plot. I had years before read some French version of one of the stories in *The Rose Garden*. She liked the idea and I wrote it out, dialogue and all. She took this and added some pretty epigrams and speeches —I called them her little liver pills—and the play was produced. To my surprise I discovered that I received absolutely no credit anywhere as her collaborator. I went to Ellen Terry and complained, but while she admitted the justice of my claim she said that to make a fuss about the matter could do no good to anyone, so I allowed the thing to drop. But imagine, that woman had the audacity to print the play without even referring to me! Finally the Lord threw her over for good and all, and one night she went to bed quietly and was dead in the morning. She had taken a dose of something. Probably suicide. One day some years afterward her mother was on the point of telling me all about it, when her father interrupted and I never learned the end of the story."

The play Moore spoke of was *Journey's End and Lovers' Meeting*. I happen to know that on the original program and in the reviews Moore *was* given credit as co-author.

At ten o'clock we walked with Moore to Catherine's studio, Cecile not yet having returned from Muriel Hueffer's. We sat talking there for an hour. Catherine showed him a reproduction of one of Zorn's recent etchings but he pushed it aside, telling us that when the Swedish artist first came to London he had seen a good deal of him. Perhaps Moore had given him the notion that he liked his etchings, several of which Zorn had later sent him. "I threw them into a drawer somewhere, and one day I looked at them and tore them to pieces.

Zorn painted and etched thousands of big naked women; he drew with facility but without real distinction."

"This little Ingres you have is exquisite. Why collect photographs of nonentities when you can buy Ingres? I wish Ingres were alive today; he would be the man to make the illustrations for *Héloïse and Abélard*. I have been looking for someone to do that. There are no longer any good illustrators. I had the greatest difficulty finding someone to draw the title-page for the new edition of my *Memoirs,* and I decided at last on a certain well-known architect, but his sketch was so badly drawn, so lacking in design, that I discarded it and took that of a young American; you will realize how well he did his work when you see the new edition of the book."

By now Moore was very tired, but with a certain old-world courtesy he managed to sit bolt upright and attend to what we were saying. At last he apologized, saying that he had much sleep to make up for; besides, his infected foot was beginning to hurt again. He slowly rose, with great dignity, in spite of his felt slippers and the purple umbrella he had tucked under his arm.

"It is clear that Mrs. Clark has been detained. Will you express to her my regret that I missed her this evening?"

Catherine and I felt a little sorry for the old gentleman, especially as he refused our offer to find a taxi for him, so he gladly took hold of our arms for the walk back to Foyot's.

The next day, Sunday, Moore came to Catherine's studio promptly at two. Cecile and I stayed upstairs in our room for an hour, as we knew Moore wanted to give Catherine the best possible chance to work. But Catherine had made me promise to come down at three, which I did. Moore was sitting motionless and silent when I came in, and scarcely looked at me. Catherine smiled, which meant that I should go away again. I tactfully bowed my way out.

Catherine passed on to me afterward the little she could

remember of their conversation. He had asked all sorts of personal questions, and once when she hesitated he smiled and said, "Don't mind an old man like me: in matters of love I am no longer a practitioner, only a diagnostician."

By shrewd and sympathetic maneuvers and some cajolery he drew her out until she gave him, as she phrased it, the "story of her life." He was impressed by the way she told it, and remarked that it would be pleasant to have a daughter like her.

"But you have, haven't you?"

"I don't know. N—— is very sweet to me, and I am fond of her. I hope she is my daughter, but I am not positive. Tell me, where did you hear about that?"

Catherine was embarrassed, because it was I who had told her this bit of gossip, repeating what Jacques Blanche had passed on to me. She didn't answer that question directly, and Moore did not press her. He had just told her that *his* life was an open book, and she might feel free to ask him anything she liked.

Catherine's drawing did not turn out well. She says she was nervous and too much absorbed in what Moore was telling her to pay much attention to her work. Moore agreed that the sketch was not right, but he gave her his criticism in gentle words.

Meantime I was writing in my room, and an hour after I had interrupted Catherine and Moore there was a light tap on the door and Moore pushed his way in. I was typing a chapter of my translation of Bordeaux's novel *La Maison morte*. Moore came to the table, picked up the book and asked what I was doing.

"Trying to earn a few dollars to pay for board and room. I was commissioned to do this job for an American publisher. Most of it's easy, but here and there I find turgid passages."

"But you can write better than Bordeaux (I wish I could!). Why waste your time? Do you write it out first in longhand?

Dear, dear. Why don't you try dictating to your wife? How long have you been at work on this?"

"About two weeks," I answered.

"Two weeks? Doesn't that interfere with your work on *Esther Waters*? I never work at more than one thing at a time, and I don't understand how you can dissipate your attention this way."

I assured him that my part of the play would be done on time and in his hands by the time he returned to London.

"As you choose, then, but mind you don't neglect the play."

He sat back on the bed, his long arms stretched out, his head touching the wall. He said he had had a long sleep, his foot felt better, and he admitted that he didn't feel quite so bitter toward Dujardin as he had felt yesterday; but he began again complaining about Hardy and Conrad; picking more and more flaws in Freeman's book and wondering why it was that someone had persuaded Freeman he was a poet. "Now everything he writes is in verse form. He was explaining to me an idea he had for a long narrative poem; someone tells the story of a prizefight to another person, and at the end it turns out that the listener is blind. I told Freeman he ought to make the blind man a former fighter, and make the scene a prize-fight. Would you believe me, Freeman thought his idea was better than mine?"

"I have a very full week of writing ahead of me: when I return to London I shall finish that confounded preface for Liveright, who is again making life miserable for me; yet he must have his preface, and it would be wrong of me to worry the life out of *him*. And when that work is done I shall look at your final version of *Esther Waters* which you tell me will be in my hands at the time agreed upon between us; and I will write you my opinion of it. But first the preface."

"I thought you had finished that at Le Val Changis? I saw a heap of typewritten pages."

"That was all wrong. I believe I have discovered the proper mood for it now; the key to my problem; I can complete the whole thing in less than a week now. It will go somewhat like this." He rose and began declaiming and walking from the bed to the window and back again, waving his arms and tasting the words as they flowed from his lips:

"My dear American friends; the time has come for me to thank you for your generous appreciation of my writings. This letter will tell you my feelings and express my gratitude. Yet no letter of twenty-five pages can possibly be filled with such expressions, and since my publisher has asked me to write a preface, I must of course say something. I will therefore tell you, for it seems to interest you to know such things, how all my books came to be written—and so on and so on, do you see? I've got the key now, the proper tone."

Sitting down again he looked at a page of the Bordeaux translation in my typewriter, and told me that he had been trying for the past three days to say in French that his "love-life is over." An old mistress had written to him and he wanted to phrase this idea poetically and correctly.

"I think it would be right to say, *Les saisons des grandes amours sont déjà passées*. What is the number and gender of *passées?*" I explained as well as I could, and then asked him how he would translate our English phrase *How often*, as in the sentence, "How often do these trains leave?"

He suggested several parallels, all of them wrong, and I told him what a Frenchman had told me: "*Tous les combiens partent-ils les trains?*" He tried to repeat this but gave up in despair. It didn't sound right to me, either.

"I am gradually losing my French," he said, "and in another five or six years I shall not be able to speak the language at all."

He insisted that I go on, then and there, with my work on the Bordeaux translation. He said he felt guilty for having intruded upon me. I unwillingly started typing, and Moore picked up a copy of a new illustrated book on Watteau.

"I don't care much now for Watteau," he interrupted, and I stopped work to look at the photogravures. "I am ahead of my time, but before you die you will find everyone agreeing with me. Look at that picture—it's silly, don't you see? Meaningless. The poses are affected; the painting factitious." And he shut the book with a bang.

Now he must be going, and I must go on with my work. Perhaps he would rest a little before dinner. He bowed his way out, and marched down the hallway.

At seven I appeared at the Voltaire, where Moore was waiting for me. We talked as much as ever, but a great deal of what we said was only variations on topics already discussed of late.

I asked about a play mentioned in one of Moore's early letters to Blanche, which Blanche had shown me recently. This made mention of a manuscript by Moore and Aléxis, that had been "accepted at the Odéon."

"There is an amusing story in that. Years ago, 1872 or '73, I made a French version of Gilbert's *Sweethearts* and sent it to the Odéon. Aléxis had gone over the French for me, and he and Zola made a few changes in the text. I heard nothing more of it until seventeen years later when Forel, the director, wrote that the play had been accepted and was actually in rehearsal. I was puzzled by the title, *Le Sycamore,* until Aléxis told me that that was what he had called it; the title I used was something like *Les Amants.* Forel's letter was forwarded from London to Paris, where I happened to be at the time, and I went to the Odéon box-office. I asked an attendant about the play, stating that M. Forel had informed me of its acceptance. The attendant, in true French fashion, consulted with half a dozen other officials, but no light was thrown on the problem. Now it happened that the Odéon was then offering a transla-

tion of the *Midsummer Night's Dream,* and evidently the man
at the door had some confused notion about this *Anglais* whose
play had been accepted by his theater, so with a grand and
sweeping gesture he waved aside a long line of patrons. 'Let
this Monsieur pass in; he may be M. Shakespeare!' My play
was badly cast and execrably staged. It ran only six or seven
nights."

At eight-thirty we took a taxi, picked up Catherine and
Cecile in the Rue Visconti and went over the River to the Li-
corne Galleries in the Rue de la Boëtie. We were early and
there was an exhibition of Futurist paintings in the foyer;
Moore carefully scrutinized every painting, made strange
grimaces at them, and said, "There is nothing here to interest
us."

The play we had come to see was acted in a small studio.
There were perhaps a hundred people present, who sat round
in comfortable arm-chairs. Moore looked at the program and
with evident disgust read out to us the title, the author's name,
and the cast of characters.

"*L'Enfant mort,* par Jane Hugard! My God, why did I
bring you nice young people to this affair! Can you ever forgive me?"

A bad performance of a dull play. Poor Moore dozed once
or twice, but he never entirely lost that bodily dignity which
seems to be a part of his character as an old-fashioned gentleman. When the curtain fell for the last time he declared he
would not wait to speak to the author, and we all hurried
downstairs and into a cab.

Catherine said she could write as good a play herself.

"Oh, no," said Moore. "Only once in a generation is it
permitted to any mortal to write a play like that! I shall tell
Dujardin just what I think of it, and say that in Jane Hugard
France has lost a good concierge."

Cecile, Catherine and I got out at the rue Visconti. Moore
was too tired to come in; besides, he was leaving for London

in the morning. He was sorry to say Goodbye, but he was sure he would see us all soon again. His long face was grave as he spoke, and he reminded me once more of the Knight of the Rueful Countenance. The taxi started with a jerk, but Moore composed himself in an instant, adjusted his brown hat, and disappeared into the shadows of the narrow street.

CARL B. CLINTON
RANDOM MEMORIES OF A FAILURE

CARL B. CLINTON

E VERY summer since I was a year old I lived at Chautauqua. *The* Chautauqua, I mean, not the tawdry travelling troupes that have used the name and made it a laughing-stock. Chautauqua was, and I imagine it still is, among other things, a place where anyone with ideas on education, art of politics might come and speak his mind; not only might, but was encouraged to do so. I know of no forum or university where there was greater freedom from restraint, and this was true not only of persons with strange or radical ideas, but of hard-shelled Fundamentalists who insist that the gates of the Hereafter are closed to all but the elect. During all the years I spent there, as a child and later as a member of the faculty, I never knew of any attempt to muzzle anyone, no matter how odd or even subversive the doctrines he preached. Negro lecturers appeared on the public platform and were guests at faculty receptions, and this long years before we began to take intelligent steps as a nation to do something about the "Negro" problem. Russian anarchists, some of them bomb-throwers, mixed in friendly comradeship with mild-mannered missionaries, and Pacifists were listened to by large audiences in wartime without too much heckling, and certainly without threat of arrest or lynching. I became used, at a very early age, to the notion that everyone with a mission, no matter how silly or dangerous it might seem, had an inalienable right to be heard. Prime ministers, Catholic priests, Rabbis, Hindu patriots, labor union organizers, political bosses, scientists and inventors with the oddest ideas, Socialists, pleaders for White Supremacy—all these we took in our stride.

(157)

It was, therefore, a matter of course that the figure of Carl B. Clinton should seem in my young eyes just another in the long procession of more or less interesting men who customarily appeared for a few days or weeks, and passed on. I first met him when I was twelve or thirteen, and my brother Bob (we did everything together then) was a little over a year younger. My memories of this man are sharp and clear, but I never took notes and the details I am setting down are all gathered from what I recall after a considerable lapse of time. I am not trying to reconstruct a chronological record, but in a series of brief flashes the impressions made on me at various times over a long period.

What Mr. Clinton did for me was to give me a love for music. It was not merely what is so often called "appreciation," which is likely to be only a number of historical and technical facts; in some strange fashion he was able to communicate something of his own passion for music to others. Just how this was done I cannot explain, but I am telling as well as I can how the process affected me. I can only now see him in some sort of perspective: when I first knew him I did not realize that he was what I later learned to call a carrier, in the medical sense. I was convinced during my early contacts with him that it was for my benefit alone that he gave so generously of himself. He was an enthusiastic, happy and eternally flowing source of infectious joy. What he had was a contagious personality, and he could not, even if he wanted to, guard others from infection.

"Mr. Clinton"—we always called him that—was about as conventional in his attitude toward life as a medieval saint. In a way there was something saint-like about him; but nothing of the ascetic or austere. He had his private objects of worship, and he was pleased when he could convert others to his way of thinking, and when he couldn't he was not distressed. Perhaps I can succeed in giving some approximate notion of the man by saying that his life, as I knew it, was one long process

of giving off. He was like Radium, and if Radium can be prodi-
gal and unthinking when it is "active," then the parallel is
more exact.

He might accurately he called a lecturer on music. At
least that was the only known source of his income. Yet this
bald statement gives no notion of what he really did, or was.
He conducted informal chatty courses in what was officially
termed "Music Appreciation," and illustrated them by playing on a Pianola. He knew personally some official of the firm
that manufactured these instruments, and was paid what he
humorously called a salary. It was probably a drawing account,
and I think that he never got a check without asking for it—
when he needed a pair of shoes or a new shirt. I remember
his telling me that the only income he was reasonably sure of
amounted to less than two dollars a day. From time to time
he accepted small fees for a lecture or a class, but I don't think
he ever turned down an invitation because the amount offered
was too small, or even when there was no cash available at all.

"Dollars," he would say, "are ludicrous and disgusting
things. An idea or an emotion is always more precious to me
than a dollar. You can't listen to dollars playing heavenly
music, can you?" No wonder Main Street thought such a fellow a nut. Well, after his own exquisite fashion, he *was* a nut.

I see him clearly now—on his six-hundred-a-year salary,
sporting a handsome Panama hat, wearing spotless duck trousers, a dark blue coat, and swinging a cane—on his way to a
lecture, or a party, or to call on some old lady who had asked
him to tea. Wherever he went he carried one or two books on
his person, or a newspaper clipping tucked inside his hat,
and on little or no provocation he would stop at a street corner to read a poem, to himself when no one else was in sight,
or to some stranger who looked as though he might care to
hear a new poem of Francis Thompson or a new metrical version of something from Guido Cavalcanti. He loved to read
as he walked, and this he would customarily do to the accom-

paniment of wide sweeping gestures, and perhaps a half-chant from Beethoven's *Ninth*, or a chorale of Bach. . . .

He was tall—well over six feet, or so he seemed to me in the early years. Well built, too, and so easy with his gestures. He invariably walked with a rolling, swinging gait. Giant strides. A long and rather narrow face; blue eyes; a pink and unlined face. He was beginning to get bald even when I first knew him, but he always managed to keep a tiny fringe of golden hair. His eyebrows were so light that a short distance away he seemed to have none at all.

He had, and so far as I know, still has, a friendly and child-like curiosity about people. If Mr. Irwin, the ancient professional fisherman known to most of us at Chautauqua as the Silent Philosopher, passed him on the street and failed to say Howdy, Mr. Clinton would pause a moment in front of him and ceremoniously greet him:

"And how are you this fine day, my dear sir? By 'fine day' I am not speaking figuratively. It *is* an amazingly fine day, isn't it? Perhaps you are not familiar with Emerson's noble lines? Or if you are, let me remind you—." If Mr. Irwin offered a smile in return that was quite enough for Mr. Clinton. Well and good, the fisherman was not at the moment to be drawn into conversation, and Mr. Clinton would take off his hat with a courtly bow and pass on, swinging his cane. Old ladies and young children in particular were attracted to him, and he treated them all with deference and respect, if not as old friends, and always managed to convey to them a part of the contagious contentment he never failed to carry with him. It seemed to me that he knew everyone, and utter strangers would usually answer his greeting as though they ought to have known him, even when they didn't. When Edison came to Chautauqua on one of his periodical visits, he would sit on the front porch of the Miller house in the early mornings, in one of those big uncomfortable rocking chairs that are usually offered to guests of honor. The old gentleman was in his customary place one day, when Mr. Clinton, with me trying to keep pace with his long strides, stopped as we were about to pass by. He looked up at the startled inventor; took off his hat and bowed. "Good morning to you, sir. Don't get up, if you please. This is merely an act of homage on our part." Though Mr. Edison had been an occasional customer of mine when I had a paper route, he hadn't the slightest notion who these strange-acting fellows could be. It was not till many years had passed that Mrs. Edison told me her husband remembered the incident, and commented on the distingushed looking giant who had somewhat startled the inventor by his unexpected, and not unpleasing, gallantry. Mr. Clinton commented to me after we had paid our obeisance that he felt sorry for anyone who would never have the pleasure of hearing music.

A happy taster of life, an adventurer in the highways and bypaths of mankind and the arts, a laughing philosopher. A voracious reader as well, a research student—after his own strange fashion—an enthusiast for most of the arts, a mixer, always good company, a wonderful raconteur. . . .

He was pleased when his classes or audiences were large, but seemed wholly unconcerned if sometimes he had only a handful of listeners. My brother and I were the only students he had in one course. This was after the summer session and most people had gone home. Mr. Clinton knew he was going to make little or nothing out of the course, but he had a couple of weeks to spare and so long as anyone at all was ready to listen to his comments and the music he had to offer, it was all right with him: he was ready to welcome even a single student. He had two—my brother and me. "Well, this is something like!" He smiled benignly, and we were off. "You two are my most faithful followers—and we don't care about class-bells, and we shan't keep an eye on the clock, shall we?" It had always hurt him, during the regular class periods in mid-summer to be forced to interrupt the playing of Bach's *Chaconne* or the

Archduke Trio when the bell rang. "*I* don't mind having to stop in the middle, but to do that to Bach is sacrilegious!" So our private class began with Beethoven's *Ninth,* and when the performance closed and the class period came to an end, he took out the roll of the first movement and put it into place again on the Pianola. "Let's play the whole thing all over again, shall we?" Bob and I preferred that to fishing, anyway, and we were happy. Meantime Jo, the Negro janitor who had been sweeping the hallway outside, stuck his head into the doorway when we had come to the middle of the last movement. At that moment Mr. Clinton caught sight of him. He stopped playing, went to the door, brought in Jo, pushed him into a chair, and started playing the movement all over again. "The Texas delegation isn't here, and we don't have that to worry about, so make yourself comfortable and listen. Didn't I tell you [this to the young Clarks] that a small class was better than a large one? I'm sure Beethoven lies easy in his grave now that our janitor is one of us. Jo [this to the janitor, who seemed happy and entirely at his ease] this music is set to the words of Shiller's immortal *Ode to Joy* and I want you to enjoy yourself with us. It's supposed to be sung, but we can imagine that." . . .

Bob and I had been exposed to a certain amount of "good" music in our home, but until Mr. Clinton and his Pianola became part of our lives, it hadn't been much more than an occasional diversion to us. Mr. Clinton's "lecturing" was neither conventional nor too "popular," nor was it unnecessarily technical. Aside from arousing and sharing our enthusiasm for the music he played, he taught us that some basic knowledge of form was a necessary condition to a more genuine appreciation than we could otherwise develop. He made us see the reason for "technique," and when we set out to learn the rudimentary elements of Sonata Form, for example, we could readily understand that music was necessarily something more than mere sounds. It was not long before we could sense the reason for structure, and even see in it a beauty that en-

hanced "mere" melody. It was not long before we could spot
the first and second themes, identify the bridging sections, recognize the recapitulation and compare a coda by Mozart with
one by Beethoven. It was great fun to ask each other such questions as how the Minuet of a Mozart string quartet became the
more elaborate scherzo in a Beethoven symphony or sonata.
We amused ourselves by identifying compositions by their
opus numbers. To this day I always speak of Beethoven's 11th
Piano Sonata as the Opus 22, and never the one in B Flat.
Watching our interest and enthusiasm grow, Mr. Clinton
liked to stop us in the street or when we were all out together
in our sailboat, and put us through some such exercise as,
"Name the keys of all the Beethoven Symphonies in order."
We were quick with our answers: "C Major, D Major, E Flat,
B Flat—." Or, it might be, "Whistle the first measures of the
opening of the introduction to the *Fourth*," or, "What's the
theme of the Fifth Fugue of the First Book of the *Well-tem-
pered Clavier?*" This was exciting for us all, but our guide
knew that even if we had been able to whistle the last movement of the *Hammerklavier* (quite a trick), but had no real
love for the music we chattered about, the bare technical facts
would have been meaningless. We all so loved the music we
heard and were beginning to know a little about, that it gave
us a tingling sensation, a sort of proprietary interest in "our"
composers to be able to discuss keys, opus numbers, and the
like. I still do it, even though my musical wife and my friends
among the professionals make fun of me.

With the help and advice of Mr. Clinton my parents
bought a Pianola for us and my brother and I would spend a
considerable part of our small earnings on Pianola rolls. We
collected the music we liked with a sort of frenzy of excitement,
and catalogued our growing library according to composers
and Opus numbers. I was invariably curious about everything
written by any composer I knew of and liked, and the Opus
numbers I did not hear played in public or weren't "cut" for

the Pianola became an obsession. Ever since I first heard Schubert's *Forellen Quintet*—which is Opus 114—I've been insistently curious about Opus 113 and Opus 115. Even when I had good reason to suppose that the unfamiliar *opera* were inferior, I wanted to be able to judge for myself. When Mr. Clinton told us that Haydn had written a hundred and twenty symphonies, he started me on a quest that has not yet ended, and never will be. There were, as I recall, only three on Pianola rolls when I heard the *Surprise* for the first time, and the mere names of some of the others still excite me. Some day I'd like to hear all the titled symphonies on a single program! What could be more delightful than a series that would include the *Passion,* the *Hen,* the *Bear,* the *Queen,* the *Drum Roll,* and the *Farewell?* To this day I buy records of any Haydn symphony I have never heard, and I have at least ninety-five to go before I shall be satisfied that the composer actually wrote the number he is credited with.

There must have been certain dangers in my systematic and frantic search for more and more music, as my astonished and perplexed parents took good care to point out. The mere collecting instinct, which I have always had, might have destroyed my passion for simply listening to music and liking it. This might easily have taken me into the bypaths of barren research. But it didn't: I know that from the very first music had become, as it has remained, a necessity. I never let my curiosity interfere with my immediate enjoyment of what music I had or what I could hear in the concert hall. Though I had to wait some years before hearing Beethoven's *Sixth,* for the first time, I played the symphonies I had in my library until I literally wore most of them out. I used to mark every roll whenever I played it, and I have proof that before I was twenty I had played Beethoven's *Fifth* over three hundred times. I was not trying to impress myself with statistical totals, I listened to music very much as an alcoholic absorbs liquor. I was unhappy and uncomfortable without it.

Of course, our parents were pleased in a way that Mr.

Clinton was giving us an enthusiastic and genuine interest in music. But it was rather unusual, if not a bit unnatural, that two otherwise healthy and normal youngsters, who went bare-footed, sold papers, sailed boats and swam two or three times a day, should occasionally spend two hours at a stretch listening to what was then, often sneeringly, called "classical" music. For one thing, I became something of a musical snob. Beethoven was my god, and my lesser divinities were his contemporaries and predecessors. Nearly all music written since the great Ludwig's death in 1826 was beneath my contempt. Chopin I respected, to a degree, and Mr. Clinton's admiration for Schumann entitled that composer to some consideration on my part, but Mendelssohn I dismissed as fit only for young ladies trying to learn to play the piano. Wagner had no attractions for me, and my mentor's opinion of him doubtless influenced my lifelong opinion that the work of the composer of the *Ring* was terribly repetitious and rather boring. Richard Strauss and Debussy, the moderns of my youth, struck me as essentially trivial. The Greats of German music filled my life with enough music at the time, and under the guidance of Mr. Clinton I eagerly got hold of several standard musical books in order to learn as much as I could about the few composers who interested me. I read the well-known treatises of Hadow, Parry, and Grove, and even tackled Thayer's *Beethoven*. At one time I prided myself on being able to reel off the names of every composition of Beethoven's, beginning with the Opus 1 Trios right through the Opus 135 Quartet, and I am not sure that I didn't memorize the posthumous *opera,* through Opus 256. I was so absorbed by Beethoven's life that I once memorized the celebrated Heiligenstadt Testament; I considered myself on intimate terms with nephew Carl and believed I could identify the *Ferne Geliebte*. I honored Beethoven on his birthdays for many years by playing four or five sonatas and at least as many symphonies on our old battered Pianola.

I am sure Mr. Clinton never took himself too seriously as

a teacher. In his own eyes he was merely the fellow who tried to throw open the "doors of heaven"—that is what he called his approach to a love for music, and that was quite enough for him. He always considered himself an amateur ("A charming word, don't you think?") He never laid down the law; he made no pretense to being an authority. He was a sower of seed. Johnny Appleseed is what I might have called him if I had heard of that walking saint at the time, and when I met Alice Meynell and her family at Mr. Clinton's urging, it was one of the Meynell boys who noted the similarity between my friend and the itinerant American of the early Nineteenth Century. The entire Meynell household were Clinton enthusiasts and had insisted on adopting him into their household, where he lived for many weeks. Through them he had come to know G. K. Chesterton and Bernard Shaw. They had all fallen under his spell. . . .

The scene is Paris. A college friend of mine and I went to call on him. That was in 1910. He sent a postal, directing us to go to the Rue Notre Dame des Champs, and ask the concierge for the *Monsieur Américain* who lived on the fourth floor back. We mounted a dingy staircase and knocked at the door. A deep base voice boomed an *Entrez, Messieurs!,* and we entered. An old-fashioned bed with a canopy stood in the middle of a dingy and decrepit room. The bed curtains were pulled back and, sitting upright, playing a violin, was Mr. Clinton, without a stitch of clothing on him. He was as dignified and serene as the Hermes of Praxiteles. "Be seated, *mes amis,* and don't say a word until I finish. Yesterday I unearthed the MS of an unfinished bourrée by Martini at the Bibliothèque nationale, and I copied it out. I am now playing it. Badly, of course, but I beg you to listen." Tears were streaming down his face. When he stopped, he carefully laid aside the violin, nodded to me, and turned to my companion. "If you have ears, my dear young sir, and paid attention to what I was playing, you will shed tears. If you withhold them for that music, I don't think I shall be able to forgive you." He said this with a smile, as though he did not insist on being taken too literally, just in case my friend chanced to be outside the fold of the elect.

Pausing a second to let the words sink in, he stood up, stretched himself and at last realized that he was naked. "You will excuse me a moment while I perform my ablutions in what the proprietor of this apartment is pleased to call the 'room of baths.' There is a pitcher there which the *bonne* leaves every morning for me. Three litres of water are my daily quota. In Paris one learns to treat water with respect." The bath took perhaps two minutes, and Mr. Clinton returned, singing, a pair of shorts in one hand, and other articles of clothing in the other. As he dressed, he displayed each article of apparel, and intoned in semi-serious fashion: "One undershirt, two francs thirty; one pair of holeless socks, one franc eighty; one fairly presentable shirt, its bosom very stiff and almost spotless—a gift from an old friend; one pair of trousers suitable for a prime minister, eleven francs; one second-hand frock coat that may once have been the property of M. Clémenceau, but cost me over forty francs.—You now behold a man of the world, ready to walk the boulevards, wearing a wardrobe that cost him, including the celluloid collar and home-made cravat, precisely one hundred and forty francs —or seven American dollars."

From under the bed, with the gesture of a magician, he drew forth a silk opera hat, only a trifle the worse for wear, put it jauntily and slightly askew over the baldest part of his skull, looked at himself in a small mirror, and walked to the door to open it. No, he wasn't really going out that way: he knew that would embarrass us. "Bless you, I was only joking. This gear I reserve for evening wear exclusively." He strode to the bed, took the hat off, dusted it and carefully put it back where it had come from.

"Follow me, gentlemen." With a flourish he threw open

the door, and we all descended the stairs. "Before we go to the delightful little café I am guiding you to in the Rue du Bac, you are going to accompany me to a shrine that is peculiarly memorable in my eyes." No one said a word while we marched in solemn procession across the Boulevard St. Germain, down toward the River and into a side street, stopping before one of those typical 18th Century yellow plastered *hotels* that abound in that part of the Left Bank. "Here," he announced solemnly, "is the place I have asked you to witness, and I am sure you will forgive me for taking you a little out of your way. Remove your hats and stand in reverent silence. You are now in the doorway of a house once inhabited by André Chenier. You will not utter a sound until I have paid proper obeisance to the shades of that illustrious poet."

The impressive ceremony ended, we all returned to the Rue du Bac. . . .

The scene is Paris again, in September 1909. The time and the place among these recollections are of no importance: Mr. Clinton's formal biography, which will never be written, would surely show that at some time before I met him for the first time he was so wholly himself that what he did and said in 1909 was as characteristic as it would be in 1905 or in 1925. I had just come to Paris as a student, and Mr. Clinton appeared—from somewhere. I don't recall. Perhaps I had known he was in the city already. At any rate he came striding into the little room I had in the home of a French family on the Boulevard du Montparnasse. "You're coming with me to the quaintest little restaurant I have found in this neighborhood, only a few steps away in the Rue du Cherche-Midi. Put on your hat, and never mind a clean collar. You'll be wearing celluloid collars as I do in a few days, and saving enough on laundry to buy extra tickets for theaters and symphony concerts. Come with me." Down the six flights of stairs we went (no *ascenseur,* of course) and straight to the quaint restaurant. There was nothing out of the way about it, and I was right in assuming that what attracted him was its cheapness and the company he had found there. It was patronized largely by coachmen who smoked those suffocating *Marylands* which I called *Coachman's Delights*. The patron welcomed us as we went in, and called at once for Marthe, the waitress, a peasant type, young, very plain and showing by her manner that *le Monsieur Américain* had made another convert. "Mademoiselle Marthe, you behold here an old and honored friend of mine, also a Monsieur Américain." This in a very formal and stilted French. "This young and, as you will perceive, very charming Monsieur has heard me sing the praises of your *Bœuf bourguignon*. You will be good enough to serve us two portions of that and a demi-bouteille of the special Beaujolais you brought me last evening." Then, to me after Marthe had disappeared into the kitchen: "Beaujolais I imagine is a wine you don't know. You should. Since you plan to spend a year in this city you will familiarize yourself with some of the characteristic French potations. I can recommend the ordinary types of Beaujolais (only with red meats, naturally), and you will find it almost as delectable as the rare vintages they serve at the *Tour d'Argent*. Those you couldn't afford, anyway. I suggest Chablis among the white wines, unless you insist on such effeminate fare as Sauternes, which is good only for American ladies of limited intelligence and no *savoir-vivre*. But enough now on the subject of wine. Wine is a noble thing if treated with respect, but you will recall Mr. Dooley's comment? 'The minyit a man relies on it for a crutch he loses the use of his legs? By the way, have I told you where we are going tonight? To the *Concert Touche,* a sixteen-piece orchestra way over on the other side of the River. They play every night and they are exceptionally good. Experienced musicians. The price of tickets is reasonable—one franc. I am sure you will become a regular customer. Tonight is a special program, Bach and Mozart. And tomorrow you shall also come with me and hear some very exceptional playing: three young men have formed a trio and I believe that one day the world will hear of them. Their names are Cortot, Thibault, and Casals. I recently heard them play a little Mozart *Divertimento* and they were heavenly—there's no other word for it.—And now to our *Bœuf bourguignon* and the Beaujolais—no, no, don't fill your glass to the top, dear boy! Let me show you, and don't *drink* it. One never *drinks* wine, one savors it, inhales it, caresses it. This must be a ceremony. Oh, dear, it will take a lot of educating to make you into a real Frenchman, but I know you have it in you to learn.—*C'est bien, ma chère.*" The waitress had hesitated a moment at our table, and Mr. Clinton addressed her because he saw she was ill at ease and wanted a word with him. Speaking loudly as though he were a coachman complaining about the service, he motioned Marthe to come close to the table. "Have no fear, Marthe, I will speak to the *patron* if he thinks you guilty of any derelection of duty.—Is it about the book I gave you last week? Ah, yes. Did you enjoy it? Have you read it all?—*Naturellement,* but you promise to finish it? *Bon, très bon!* I can assure you that the story will speak to your heart, and when you have finished the last page, tell me when I next come here. At that time I shall present you with another story, by the great Norman writer Gustave Flaubert —You never heard of him? Tch, tch, I am just a little ashamed of you, and you from Rouen, too, like Flaubert!—You perceive we have finished our meat course and we are now ready for dessert. What have you to suggest for us?—A *Petit Suisse?* Excellent, with some of that delicious apricot confiture mixed with blanched almonds." The cheese was not to my taste, but I liked the confiture. Since it would not do to hurt Marthe's feelings, Mr. Clinton ate my *Suisse.* After demi-tasses of what was supposed to be coffee, Mr. Clinton lighted a cigar and we left the café. The modest tip for Marthe and the four sous spent for the cigar left nothing for bus fare, so the two of us had to walk all the way across town, a matter of three miles before we reached the Boulevard Sébastopol, where the

Touche orchestra was located. Paris was new to me then, and
I remember only that my guide pointed out house after house
where some artist, or writer, or composer, had lived. . . . "Ah,
here we are. Gluck composed his *Armide* in that room. Do
you like Gluck? Exactly what I feel—in small doses, and only
on special occasions. And now here is Bizet's house, and over
there Massenet's. Maybe we can catch a glimpse of the old fellow now—see the light in his room? From that window he can
see most of the Luxembourg Gardens.—Come, let's spend no
more time on him. I know you don't care for his music any
more than I do.—Now we are in the neighborhood of some of
the great Revolutionary figures. This is where Danton's house
used to stand, and here—in the Café Voltaire building—is
where Desmoulins lived with his lovely wife. And down that
street Marat was murdered by Charlotte Corday. However, he
doesn't interest me at all. Desmoulins was a fine figure of a
man and I would not be surprised to learn that he played the
flute. You can hardly imagine that of Marat, can you? But we
must hurry now or we shall miss Mozart's *Harp Concerto,* but
I do want you to look at that church—*St. Julien-le-Pauvre:*
Dante is said to have attended services there when he was a
student at the University. . . .

The concert began, under the direction of the expert M.
Touche, an undersized cellist with a long black beard. The
audience sat at small tables, where coffee and beer were served
by discreet waiters who were never allowed to serve while the
music was being played. Our waiter, of course a friend of Mr.
Clinton, greeted us with friendly attention, and my guide introduced me. "A future customer of yours, Pierre. I assure you
he will attend your concerts—yours, that is, and M. Touche's
—so long as the programs remain as excellent as they usually
are. But I warn you not to expect him here when you offer too
much Wagner, or Massenet. I count upon you to see to it that
he is constantly provided with generous doses of Beethoven
and Bach, which may be delicately balanced by a fair share of

Haydn and Mozart, and perhaps with a few of the Romantics, especially Schubert and Schumann. I will also settle for a sampling of your French composers. No Berlioz, please, however."

The orchestra was good, considering that they rarely or never had time to rehearse, gave at least eight different programs every week, and all the members were certified as having received first prizes at the Paris Conservatoire. The Bach on this first evening was mostly unfamiliar to me, and I looked forward in particular to the famous Concerto for Two Violins. Mr. Clinton had often lectured on it, and even played stray themes from it on his violin. But just after the intermission and before the Concerto was about to begin, he rose from our table and whispered: "I am going out to smoke during this number. Don't worry; I'm not ill. You will of course remain. The second movement will transport you to Paradise. I shall return after the last movement. You see, I have never heard this Concerto performed, and I never intend to while I live. That is one of the few compositions I am saving up for the after-life. *A bientot!*

This struck me as strange at the time, but in a way I must have known then, as I came to believe later, that he will never be bored when he goes to his Great Reward. There will be plenty of Bach for him to enjoy.

After the Concerto ended, the tall figure of Mr. Clinton strode into the hall again, ready to listen to the three *Brandenburg Concerti* which were next on the program. "Wasn't it glorious, I ask you?", speaking of the Concerto he had refused to listen to. I've never enjoyed thinking about it so much before, but the second movement must have been a trifle slow? I timed the whole thing, and it should not have taken over twenty-seven minutes."

. . . . I had seen him by chance in London the following spring, and besides taking me to call on an ex-pugilist who had taken up poetry as a profession, and kneeling with him on the doorstep of a house in Russell Square, where a "very beautiful woman" he knew had once lived, I have no recollection of being with him again for several years. He would disappear at times as suddenly as he turned up; but he would always manage, wherever he was, to send his friends post cards or clippings from papers and magazines that interested him. There was no telling what he would be doing next, or where he had settled down, but wherever he happened to be he was sure to have found friends, and when he was alone, he would make friends with cathedrals, or paintings, birds or animals. Picture post-cards would come to me, decorated in the margins with crude drawings of himself in front of St. Mark's in Venice feeding the pigeons, or a cartoon of himself seated at some small café in Bruges or Linz. One card from Madrid told how he had wasted his life because he had only discovered, after reaching the age of forty, the full glory of the Velasquez portraits in the Prado, and that Goya had been a closed book to him until that very moment. And again, a short note from Perugia where he had been given for his use a corner of the sacristy in an abandoned church. It was from Orvieto that he announced, in Pontifical Italian mixed with French, that he was about to complete his fabulous life's work, a book on the *Appreciation of Music*. I had heard about that for years, how it would revolutionize the entire approach to the understanding and love of music, and when I was still in my teens I had sat in wonderment as its author read passages from the immense heap of pages that he invariably took with him wherever he went. The work actually was set up in page-proofs (at Mr. Clinton's expense), but somehow the publishers remained uninterested. The world waited long years for the masterpiece, but Mr. Clinton was apparently unwilling to put the necessary finishing touches on it. Publishers had seen parts from time to time, but I don't think any one of them ever offered a contract. The years passed, but I never saw the slightest sign of disappointment or discouragement on Mr. Clinton's face.

Once, after I had begun to suspect that something was wrong somewhere, I told Mr. Clinton that possibly his gift to the world was not to be, perhaps should not be, through the printed word, but lay rather in the warmth and humanity of Clinton, the human being. Maybe he simply lacked the technical means for communicating his ideas to others except by word of mouth. I went on to tell him, more directly and openly than I had ever before ventured to do, that I looked upon him rather as a kind of St. Francis of the arts than as a mere writer of books. I had never come so near saying how deeply he affected me and how he must have affected so many others. He was embarrassed, and he blushed all over his face and neck and the bald dome of his shapely head. Naturally, he was pleased, but he couldn't bring himself to say so. He took refuge, as he often did when ill at ease, in quoting one of his beloved authors. It may have been something from Emerson; but I know he quoted Mr. Dooley: "It's unsafe fer anny man alive to receive the kind words that ought to be said only iv the dead." And that was all.

. . .I have heard people call him a failure, a frustrated artist who took refuge in dabbling in the arts and wasting time that should have been put to far better use. Close friends of his time and again urged him to capitalize on his charm and I know of one man who offered to subsidize the publication of his book. Mr. Clinton would appear to consider such suggestions seriously for a moment, and then burst into a broad smile, and say, "What is success anyway? I've seen so many examples of it and it seems to me a pretty dreary thing. I'm content with my lot. Who has better friends than I? The people I know, the books I read, and the music I can listen to. If my life is a failure, so be it. I have no complaint to make."

But the hard-headed "successes," the practical business men, strangely, did not always scorn his impracticality; there were many who accepted him on his own terms. Once, at Chautauqua, after giving a lecture on Beethoven, he was approached by an insurance salesman who assured him he could easily be trained to "sell" anything, meaning in this case insurance. Mr. Clinton put his arm round the man's shoulder, and with a disarming smile, said, "If I have been able to sell you on Beethoven, that's all I ask." "I won't say you sold me on Beethoven, though you made him sound interesting, but you did sell me on Clinton. But wouldn't you like to make money?" "No, sir, I would not. To begin with, I wouldn't have any idea what to do with it if I did, and besides I already earn the little money I really need. I have unlimited wealth of another kind: the heart and soul of the world are at my disposal and I pay nothing for them—no money, that is. And all mankind is my friend. What more can any man ask? Nevertheless, I must thank you for coming to the lecture, my dear sir." There was not a trace of any contempt for the friendly Babbitt. As a matter of fact, I never heard him say a serious word in disparagement of anyone's opinions or way of life. In one sense, he seemed to me at times to have no discrimination in choosing his friends or companions. He would often ask me to go with him and meet "a most wonderful and beautiful woman," who as likely as not might turn out to be utterly commonplace in appearance. He was by no means unaffected by the attentions of young and attractive women, but he seemed to get just as much pleasure from the company of the most unattractive hags. So long as he could receive or communicate anything in any human relationship, that was enough for him. He had known James Huneker years before at the Players Club in New York, and the two had presumably found much in common to talk about; I have already mentioned his relations with Shaw and Chesterton; years before I met him he used to give Thanksgiving and Christmas parties to the newsboys in his neighborhood in New York; I have seen him sitting on sandpiles telling stories to young children, and heard him tell with delight of going into the kitchens of large hotels and chatting with cooks and servants. There was, so far as I could learn, no deliberate effort on his part to "improve" anyone, and he would have been amazed and abashed if anyone had thought his attitude patronizing. I am quite sure that if he were to find himself suddenly transported to the heart of Darkest Africa he would feel utterly at home, and before long he would have converted the savages to the beauties of Bach and Beethoven and Emerson, and possibly drilled them to sing choruses from *The Messiah....*

I shudder to think what dreadful meanings the modern analysts of the soul would make of what I have said about him, but what I have written was set down long before Psychoanalysis became fashionable. The matter would not have occurred to me, and never did, until I considered the evidence I have set down in these pages in all its horrible nakedness. But being something of a sceptic over the way thoughts and actions are interpreted by some of the experts, I have little doubt that Mr. Clinton would be characterized as a monster with all sorts of unresolved suppressions, a menace to society and a horrible example of something. If he was in any way abnormal and a menace, I shall have to alter all my notions of what a normal life should be; at any rate, his is the sort of abnormality I admire enormously. His oddities appear to me now as necessary ingredients in a man who thought it odd that his fellow-beings, with eyes to see with and ears to hear with, are missing most of life that is worth-while....

The last time I visited him was in New York. He had a large room in one of those old houses that used to stand on the South side of Washington Square. The place had not been cleaned or swept since the days John La Farge had lived there, and it was a mess of books, sheet music, old clothes, scattered bedding, and half a dozen modern reproductions of 17th and 18th Century stringed instruments: harpsichords, clavichords, spinets and the like. "See," he announced, taking my wife around the room. (This was the first time he had met her.) "You will be interested in these, I'm sure," he said as he pointed out each instrument. "By the way," he went on, "my heartiest felicitations, Barrett. You have married not only a pianist, but a very beautiful young woman. And now, my dear lady, will you show me how to finger this Bach *Partita?*" Where he had got the instruments I don't remember; they had probably been loaned to him by the Pleyel or Gaveau piano people, who had then recently begun putting such things on the market. He had been trying to play the old music on the kind of instruments it had been written for, and this experience had necessitated another drastic revision in the Big Book. "You will be pleased to learn that the magnum opus is nearly ready. I have only two chapters that require touching up now, and then I have to work up that Bill for Congress. You will recall that I once decided to put all of it into the appendix. Long ago I told you I got a Senator who was a friend of mine to introduce a bill for the establishment of an Office of Music Appreciation in the Federal government. I wrote it myself and it runs to over a hundred pages. Some day I hope that that, at least, will be published—in the Congressional Record!—Look at this, if you will, both of you. It's part of a cantata I found in an old book store on Fourth Avenue the other day; it's supposed to be something of Vivaldi's, but it sounds a little early for him, what do you think?" . . . It was not long till the conversation began to lag; Mr. Clinton seemed tired, and something of his old gaiety had gone. He looked rather shabby, too, and his trousers needed pressing, and his shirt cuffs were frayed. My wife was uneasy, I know, and if she had known him better she would have offered to mend his socks. For the first time I was conscious that this man was beginning to grow old, that he might possibly be in need of money, but when we were ready to leave, he went with us to the door and I think he may have had an impulse to throw his arms around us. But, if so, he restrained himself. I also think he realized something of what was on my mind, and to put me at my ease, he smiled broadly and turning to my wife, "Your good husband," he said, "knows that his old friend Clinton is not entirely himself unless he quotes Mr. Dooley. You will doubtless recall the paper on education, and the passage that goes something like this: 'In the college where these studies are taught it's understood that even better than gettin' the civic ideal is bein' head of a trust.' Well, my ideals may not be civic in any narrow sense, but I am head of a trust. My trust is not limited in its membership except for those who don't care to join. It's a trust that gives and doesn't take. So much for philosophy, my dear friends. Bless you!"

. . . Only a short time ago, years after the visit to Washington Square, I watched a slightly bent figure walking slowly up Sixth Avenue, wearing an outmoded frock coat, and leaning on what had once been a smart-looking cane. The cane was rather a necessity than the symbol of that unruffled happiness I had for many years known it to be. But though the outward bearing of the man was changed there was something in his unlined cheeks and forehead and the unchanged blue of his eyes that proved to me that Mr. Clinton's contentment with the world of men had not changed. The dollars he might have earned would have brought him only annoyance, and he would have regretted the misspent years as irrevocably lost. He had something within him that was his because he had shared it, and I repeated to myself one of his favorite quotations: "The gift is to the giver." He passed me by without seeing me, and somehow I was sure that of all the men I had ever known he was the happiest, and the most successful.

SIDNEY HOWARD
IN HIS LETTERS

SIDNEY HOWARD

A few days after the funeral at Tyringham I was asked to speak about Sidney Howard over the radio. A regular program had been shifted at the last moment to allow the presentation of two scenes from *The Silver Cord*. Selena Royle, Mildred Natwick and Earle Larrimore read the principal roles and I tried in the space of six minutes to convey something of the impression made upon me by the author of that play during the many years I had known him. Like others who have since told me of the effect on them of the untimely death of this man, I wanted to tell anyone who would listen all that I could remember of him; yet to compress that into half a dozen paragraphs seemed hopeless. To make matters worse, we were scheduled to broadcast on the eve of what promised, and turned out to be, a historic climax to years of European chaos. The day we met in the studio was Sunday, September 2, 1940; the Prime Ministers of Europe and King George had already spoken, and thirty minutes after we were through the President of the United States was on the air. What I had to say could not possibly have interested more than a tiny fraction of the listening millions who had learned, only a few hours before, that another world conflict had begun; yet, even at that time—above all at that time—I knew that Sidney Howard and what he symbolized were important, that the words I spoke, because they did in a way express something of his spirit, and the words of his play so sincerely and beautifully spoken by our cast, really mattered, much more than they would have mattered under ordinary circumstances. He was to me a kind of modern knight, a man whose heart demanded, as one of his friends had said, "that there be decency and justice in the world." While writing my introductory address I could hear the tone and accent of his speech, and I found myself forming sentences as I think he would have formed them, some of them coming to me out of letters that I had not read for fifteen or twenty years.

Here, except for the restoration of a word or two I had to cut out of deference to the radio code, is what I said:

I cannot think of Sidney Howard in the past tense: I never knew any man who was so utterly alive. The mere fact of his presence among us, even the comforting knowledge that he was somewhere working, or playing, or tending his garden, was enough to renew one's courage in moments of doubt. He was to me a symbol of the fundamental sanity of things. The tall figure, habitually dressed in gray tweeds, the blue eyes that looked through you, the musical voice, that queer habit of sudden silences, his startling way of throwing an idea at you when you least expected it—such are a few of my impressions of the physical man.

But these bare words can't convey much—so let me try again: the scene is my office. He has come to meet a promising young writer whose play I had sent him the day before. 'I like your show,' he shot at the young man. 'You need cash? Sure you do. I'll let you have some. Lunch with me today—one o'clock—Harvard Club.' Next morning the boy had a job. How characteristic this swift course of action! Impulse, decision, action: that was his way. Of all the letters he wrote me few were dated: yesterday and tomorrow somehow didn't seem to exist.

Now one more memory: he had come to our home in the country one weekend to finish a play. He sat in a large wing-chair near the window, a script in one hand and a pad of note-paper in the other. My young daughters sat on the floor before him, playing. My wife and I urged "Uncle Sidney," as the youngsters called him, to shoo them away if they bothered him, but Uncle Sidney only looked at us solemnly, picked up the younger child and plumped her on his knee. She lay happily half an hour as her big friend went on working. His silence spoke to us: "I love children, and you know it blame well. If I want these kids sitting all over me, that's my headache!"

His love of children was only a part of his abounding love of the whole visible, tangible, exciting world. He enjoyed, heard, touched, felt life more passionately than any other man I ever knew. He could not weigh the practical consequences of any action once he had made up his mind to pursue it; he didn't know the meaning of tact as that word is commonly understood; he was no diplomat, and time and again, in his big simple fashion he antagonized those who couldn't understand his way. He was without mental reservations. Something needed doing; how shall we do it? Let's do it. That is how his mind worked.

I first met him twenty years ago on his return from France, where he had seen active service as captain of an air bombing squadron. The War over, he needed to be up and doing. In twenty-four hours we had started writing a play together; in another twenty-four we had begun fighting against the suppression of *Jurgen,* and in intervals, at his apartment, we were arguing over the merits of ancient Persian music, modern German painting, and American beer. The writing of that play, incidentally, proved to me that he was a playwright, and I was not.

Of his amazing activities what can I hope to say? He was a gifted linguist; he wrote respectable verse and short stories; he investigated the labor spy racket and the narcotics ring; he reviewed books, plays and pictures; he was always in the vanguard against every threat to freedom of thought or expression. After he got into his stride as a successful playwright his interests were more directly focussed upon the theater, and it was inevitable that a man with his capacity for leadership should find himself in the thick of every fight affecting the welfare of the playwright. As president of the Dramatists' Guild during a critical period of its existence, he sacrificed two years of his time and led his fellow workers to victory.

Sidney Howard would have been the first to laugh at me for trying to make him out a hero or a saint. Let me tell you then about his failings; his almost blatant sincerity often led him into conflict with others; and he had the gift of flaming anger. Once, long ago, he was furious with me; but some good instinct prompted me to stand up to him. Next day he stalked into my office, looking a foot taller than usual; silently he lifted me out of my chair, took me across the street, sat me down at the bar, and with a shy smile I could not resist, said quietly, "Howard was wrong, I guess." (That was an amusing trick of his, calling himself Howard: it was as near as he ever came to being devious!) He rarely said thank you, or acknowledged a letter—not when you expected it, but a week or a year later he would remind you and convey, with an exquisite if belated sense of fitness, his gratitude. Such were the only weaknesses of this man that I ever saw. He may have had others—in a way I hope he had.

The irrelevant and meaningless accident that killed him a few days ago just before his new comedy was to go into rehearsal ('Damn bad playwriting,' is what he would have called it), has indeed deprived those closest to him of his bodily presence, and in the face of this personal tragedy there is nothing I can say. If this man had not been able, through his art, to communicate something of his radiant personality to the world, there would be no point in my speaking about him at all. I believe that Sidney Howard would have given us finer plays than any he had yet written, but we cannot be sure. We do know, however, that he became one of the leaders of our new adult American drama, brought it vigor, honesty, intelligence, and beauty, by impressing upon it the mark of his own character: we can feel on every page he wrote the clear and steady wind of freedom that gave him sustenance. Each of his plays was born of a powerful impulse to capture living men and women and throw them (as he once phrased it) alive into the theater. In his work we can see and feel and hear the playwright proclaiming aloud his faith in the integrity and dignity of the human animal.

I believe that those of us who through him shared some of his inexhaustible love of life will agree that to him more than to most men it was given to communicate to all who have ears to listen some precious part of what made him what he was.

When I came home at midnight from the studio I went to my files and got out the Sidney Howard folder. I read a hundred pages of letters and notes, some of them written in that nervous, strong and often nearly illegible handwriting of his; some on yellow copy paper he had hurriedly typed himself; several on telegraph blanks, hotel stationery, backs of envelopes; a few that had been dictated, neatly typed and dated. Here in one bundle were nearly all of his communications from the day before we first met in 1919 until a couple of weeks before his death. A school friend of mine had known him during the early years of the War at Harvard, and had bored me with his talk about this "wonderful Sid Howard, one of the swellest men I've ever seen." My wife and I had even accused Billy Merrill of inventing an imaginary hero just to impress us.

One day after the War was over I got a note from the fabulous Howard. He had seen Billy shortly before the latter's death in Coblenz (he was with the Army of Occupation) and had promised to look me up. Howard, too, had been in the army, was in fact an air ace.

He suggested lunch at Browne's Chop House. I was of course ready to be disappointed, but that evening at home I reported that Billy had been right about his marvelous friend. It was at this first meeting that Sidney shot at me one of those characteristic questions that was not so much a question as a forthright statement:

"Do you think there's a play in *The Rivet in Grandfather's Neck?*" That was a novel of Cabell's, and in the fall of 1919 a lot of us were tremendously worked up over *Jurgen* and its author. What this Howard fellow really meant, only I didn't know it at the time, was that he was damn sure there *was* a play in *The Rivet* and he was going to get it out. I said I'd think it over.

"Think quick," he said, "and let's lunch here again tomorrow. If the answer is 'Yes,' we'll write the play together."

I re-read the novel, and we agreed to go ahead with the play.

I have nearly all the letters Sidney wrote me from that

day on, and from this point I am going to let them tell the story, with as little comment of my own as they may need. It is hardly necessary to point out that these letters are not "literary" productions. I don't think Sidney ever thought of a letter of his as anything but a swift and direct means of communication. I leave them all as they were written, correcting now and then only what are clearly slips of the pen or typewriter. As I said in my radio address, he rarely dated a letter, and most of the dates I have put in are from my own notations at the time.

The first one in my file was written shortly after we began work on the play, toward the end of 1919:

> I am taking the manuscript with me. I shall probably have time to get my ideas down upon paper while I am in Cambridge and to send you the first two sets. I shall be with [Walter Prichard] Eaton who lives in peace with only his typewriter. I don't see why I shouldn't make use of his typewriter . . .

He didn't stay long in Cambridge, and on his return to town he worked so fast I soon saw I couldn't keep up with him. I have several letters and wires urging changes of lines or situations, and I recall one phone message delivered at my office to a startled secretary, something about "let's not kill Agatha yet."

> Suggest following reforms in act I. (1) Curtain finds Colonel and Charteris going over some old wills and letters. The scene may go on much as per MS except that at the end we are told that Charteris is to work on the letters. (2) Patricia's entrance . . . cut down by Roger. The Colonel won't go out until his sister has come down. Remove lines about rivet and save them for 2nd act *but* have the Colonel tell the whole rivet story to Roger in act I. It doesn't go worth a damn in act II. Too slow during so much action. (3) Bring Agatha in with a good line on the end of the story and *alone* so that Patricia and the Colonel adjust her pillows in the chaise longue. Then close the door on the porch. Virginia can open it later.

Virginia might bring Agatha a drink. The point is to give Anne and Charteris a few lines about Agatha on stage alone *while* Pat and Col are with Agatha on porch. From then on O. K. I think there is enough in I sans rivets except in reference. See you Tuesday.

We had evidently promised to send Cabell our MS, and I know that the novelist had given us the necessary authorization together with his benediction, but the authors of the play had hesitated to send him the script. I think we were a little afraid he might be annoyed over the liberties we had taken with his story and dialogue:

> Best have the thing typed for Cabell's reading as it stands. I have gone over it very clearly. Further clarification of issues will only change them. I can't feel that the lines you added to the end of the first act helped it any except to define the allegory, which means nothing anyway. You might go over it once again. But for God's sake let's have it typed by Monday, cost what it may.

On May 28, 1920, I heard from Cabell—a gracious and courtly letter. He was still, he wrote, "in a whirl of amazement and admiration over this miracle which you and Mr. Howard have wrought. The thing is certainly a play, and to my partial judgment a very good play; and there was certainly no play in the novel." He did, nevertheless, wonder why we had done this or that, and added, "I was a bit taken aback by the talk between Charteris and Musgrave in the last act, which in the book hinges almost entirely on the fact that both men know Patricia is listening . . . [that] was robbed of its pivot; and further aback, when I saw it seemed to move quite as well without this factor. . . . Trifles, these, of course; what matters is your clever combination of Anne-Clarice, and your development of Virginia and Agatha."

The day after Sid and I agreed that we could (and would) do no more on the MS until it was sold, he wrote me this little note:

Whatever disappointing end our drama may come to, this much can be said for it—that you and I have collaborated and that our relations are still seemingly friendly both socially and professionally. Probably you realize how extraordinary that is. I asked Mother about it. She says that one of two things must be true—that you are a marvel or that I have improved, and she sees no sign of an improvement. Wherefore—Salut! It has been a damned educational and agreeable experience for me.

And then we started on the long job of finding a producer. The three following notes are taken from among a dozen of their kind:

> There is immediate prospect of a contract for the Rivet—production next Sept. . . . call me up—I want a copy of our letter to Cabell in re terms.

> Trevor turned us down on the conviction that there is no money in the show. It has gone on to Holbrook Blinn and Grace George.

> It seems foolish to report again on the Rivet but Grace George and Harris are now jumping about in their skins. I have some new hope. Meanwhile a new farce is just completed. Yours for industry.

It was at last sold to Frank Conroy. Harold Freedman was the agent who put through the deal, and it was he who handled Sidney's literary work to the very end. Then followed the usual difficulties and delays, and in the end, no production. The rest of the story is best told in this place, though it carries us forward a few years.

It was in 1926 that I looked again at the MS: I had a notion that with some rewriting it might be turned into a saleable property. The Beechwood Players at Scarborough-on-Hudson, under the expert direction of Knowles Entrikin, were interested, partly I'm sure because I was on the Board and some local interest could be stimulated among our subscribers. Of course I wanted my collaborator to work over the MS with me, but it will be seen from the next letters that he didn't think it worth while. I suspected this at the time, and I was sure of it later.

The first of this group of notes is dated March 25th, 1927:

> It is an age since I have looked at *The Rivet in Grand-father's Neck,* but I am fairly certain that it has no chance as it now stands. The Vanderlip people [i.e., the Beechwood Players: the Vanderlips had built the theatre as part of the Scarborough School] have been after it and . . . wanted me to do some work on it and put it in shape and God knows I'd be glad to do just that and get it on, but, as it stands, I'm certain it's impossible. I haven't worked on it because . . . I no longer believe the story. I'll fish a copy out and read it the first moment I get. Conroy has no rights. The play is absolutely ours unless Cabell kicks up anything of a fuss.

The reference to a fuss meant only "in case Cabell doesn't want the play done now." I wrote Cabell again at the time and he was as gracious and friendly as he had been before.

The next letter was in answer to my note insisting that our original collaboration agreement should stand unaltered.

> I daresay *The Rivet* has great possibilities. When I last read it I thought so. But I couldn't believe in it as it was and I couldn't seem to get worked up to working on it again. Now I don't agree with you that I did anything valuable on the play and for God's sake forget about that ancient contract if you have any ideas for improvements. My reputation would not suffer from anything you approved. . . . I'd be proud to advise you—for what my advice may be worth—but you had better go ahead entirely on your own and just take anything that I put in that may seem of value to you. . . . As far as I can see, I have fallen down on my job as a collaborator. It isn't the first time. Don't hold it against me.

There was not much of an argument, because I wanted to divide all income with Sid, and he insisted that the play was mine, since I did the work (which was untrue). The thing

never came to an issue because the play was never professionally produced. The last of this group of letters was written in
April 1927:

> That's a very nice letter and very like you. I don't for the
> life of me see where I have any right to any connection with
> that play. What work I did on it, I did before I knew beans
> about writing plays—Not that I know more than one or two
> beans now—and I went cold on it and simply could not con-
> tribute a damned thing. It isn't that I don't want to be respon-
> sible, but that if you put my name on it, my name having got
> the silly advertisement it has, people are bound to talk as
> though I had done a lot and I haven't. If the play comes off,
> it will be your work entirely, and I hereby, without coercion,
> recognize that fact and . . . waive all rights, if any still exist,
> in that old contract. The play is yours and good luck to it and
> I should like to see it and I hope to God it comes on to Broad-
> way and makes you and Cecile one hundred and eighty five
> thousand dollars and what a son of a—there, there!—I should
> be to butt in at all except, if you ask me to a performance, to
> tell you what I think just as you tell me what you think about
> my plays. You're a grand man as well as a grand witness.

The last phrase, referring to a plagiarism case, is explained in another letter. I had asked him to come and see the
revamped *Rivet,* on which Entrikin had made me work like a
dog. Knowles held me a prisoner in his apartment until I had,
with all sorts of help and scolding from him, turned out a
new last act, and thoroughly revised the other two. *The House
of Musgrave,* as we re-christened it, got over fairly well, and
had the customary run of three nights. Sidney had not actually
promised to attend, and he didn't want to, but he had half-
heartedly told me he might come out.

> I was out in Oyster Bay with Rob Wood for a couple of
> days and missed out on the Scarborough enterprise through
> having another engagement. I am more than sorry. For the
> next time, please and forgive me. Can we make the visit in any
> case? I do want to come out and there doesn't seem to be any
> good reason why I shouldn't come anyway on Tuesday and see

Cecile and keep you up later than a commuter has any right to stay up. And I have such a gorgeous idea for a play for Doris Keane, said idea having been inspired, as they say, by none other than Richard Myers. I must talk with you about it.

I should like to say something here about Dick Myers— the joyous and talented Dick whom Billy Merrill had introduced to Sidney in France during the War—but he enters this narrative only incidentally.

During the late twenties I was reviewing plays for a small theater magazine and it was my business to write up the Scarborough production. I enjoyed the acting, and Entrikin did wonders as a director. Since I was credited on the program as being sole author, I felt more than ordinarily free to say what I didn't like about it. My concluding sentence was, "If Mr. Clark would only forget what he knows about technique and sit down and write what he knows about people, he might turn out a play far better than this first attempt. He is never weary of telling other dramatists to do this very thing."

It was this notice that prompted Sidney to tell me in a letter from London that he knew I was a damn good critic because I saw how rotten "my" play was:

> I have been meaning to write you my felicitations on your review of The Musgrave Family. I found it and read it and loved it. I wished that the play had pleased you more but your method of reviewing it certainly pleased me. The Silver Cord goes on to packed houses in London. I am taking the Myers family back with me on Wednesday. God knows when I shall be in New York again. Bless you and the family. Haste and affection.

And that was the end of *The Rivet*.

In re-reading the next few letters I can't help wondering again at the amazing number of things that could engage Sid's attention and interest, and the amount of work he was able to do. Of course the letters to me reflect only a small part of his activities, and there are long gaps between these, as there were long periods when I did not see him at all.

Though he had written pageants, like *Lexington,* and a mask that was put on under Sam Hume's direction in Michigan, his first professionally produced play was the romantic drama *Swords,* which opened at the National Theater in September 1921. This was written for Clare Eames, whom he married shortly afterward. But even before *Swords* he had written a farce, *Ride a Cock Horse,* which I thought pretty good. As a matter of fact I told Sidney at the time, "You and I will never write another play together: *you're* a playwright." But Arthur Hopkins had remarked (and that was his only comment), "I don't believe it." "Arthur is right," Sidney said, and a year later he destroyed the script: "It's just no good, Barrett."

The next letter reached me in Berlin. I had seen a good deal of Hugo von Hofmannsthal at Salzburg and later on in Berlin; and I had the idea of translating or adapting his new play, the *Grosse Welt-Theater,* which Reinhardt had recently put on at Salzburg. The Austrian poet was one of the many victims of the economic chaos which settled over Central Europe during 1922–3 when my wife and I lived abroad. I had induced him to write an article for the *New Freeman.*

Feeling that I was incapable of rendering the soft Italianate verse of the poet into an appropriate English equivalent I suggested that Sidney do the job, and had urged him to send a copy of *Swords* to Hofmannsthal:

> I have two letters to answer you. This about Hofmannsthal arrives à l'instant. I am something loath to undertake sending him *Swords.* I shall send it rather to you. But I am so grateful for your good opinion and all that. I should have been abroad this summer on my honeymoon but I stayed home to prepare a script of my adaptation of Sudermann's *Das Blumenboot* for production in English. It was done on order for Robert Milton who had filled Sudermann with the well-known guff. It came out very well but Milton is not serious in the French sense. Then Sheldon and I did a real job called "Bewitched," which is a Freudian Fairy Tale. We can't find any actress who isn't horrified of the part. She plays a

young sorceress, an American girl of the boy's past in the beau monde, the boy's mother, a symbolic figure of sex appeal as such, and a young French girl. I can't make the notion very clear in summary but it is this—that a man expects the woman he loves to embody all the appeal of all kinds of women, flame, mother and mistress . . . and still to meet him on his own ground and if she can't do that, she bores him. So that, though you never see the real girl until the last page of the play and have no notion of how she will fare with the 100% male, you meet all her appeals to him in sequence and (in the sorceress) in combination. I should almost be inclined to send you that along with *Swords,* for it is a much more original play and much more in my line. I project three more—one laid on a California ranch; one a modern comedy and one on St. Francis of Assisi. I'll give that last to Moissi if he'll do it. For the present, being married and gloriously happy and ingloriously broke I am journalizing on politics and prohibition for N. Hapgood (and, thus, indirectly for Hearst) and writing the book page (*very* boring) on Life. How I wish I were with you and Cecile in Berlin or anywhere! . . . Clare yells that I am to ask you if you remember her at the Lyceum Theater and, if you do, sends her love. And so do I, to you both, and to little Nancy.

The next letter was likewise written before the one printed above, but it belongs in this place. It reached us in Paris a few weeks after we arrived there in December of 1921. Just before we sailed Sidney had been full of a new idea—a play about the singer Augusta Holmès, and had asked me to send him all the dope on her I could lay hands on. I had picked up a few books in which La Holmès was mentioned, and sent on George Moore's personal remark (he had called on us and I asked him about the lady), that *he* couldn't see a play in her whole damn life history.

Barrett and Cecile old dears—The books arrived upon my bed of pain this morning and have pulled me through another day of this beastly flu. I'm glad to have Villiers who is an agreeable old bore always. The filthy minded old prude who wrote the brochure does nothing but hint at Augusta's immoralities—which are the dramatic things. I am still intrigued by her. He gives me a bibliography, all about how she imitated Wagner, no doubt. I want to know who had her night key beside her maid. "Why do they all take the night boat to Albany?" No! No!! No!!! you must NOT be rough, Howard. I shall come abroad and talk to all of her ex-lovers now living. There is Mendes and a man in England and G. Moore and Renaud (whom I know). She's a person and there's a play in her. I know because I know how to end it! You are angels to have sent me all this about Augusta. I have learned a great deal already from it. But you haven't sent me your letter about Paris before and after. I want to know! I want to hear how things seem to you and how they hold water, if the Seine still flows in the right direction, if the food is satisfactory, if you are generally as happy as you should be. The *S. S. Tenacity* opened badly but has held its own tenaciously without being a very marked success. It had wonderful reviews. *Sancho* is promised for March 1 but I don't believe it. ———— [title of play?] will be tried out in April. . . . I am going to work on some new things. Just what I don't know. How my engagement burst upon you I don't know. I doubt if you were much astounded. It's gone on for so long. I intended telling you about it the last time I was at Briarcliff but I lost my nerve. I wasn't made to be autobiographical. Well, there it is. You may see Clare and me in Paris by May. I'm hoping that she will be acting in London for a while. I want to see her make a reputation there and then come home to play as a famous person. But she doesn't seem to give much of a damn. My best to Dick and Alice Lee. Lord love you both. I do.

S. S. Tenacity and *Sancho* are plays adapted by Sidney; the first was written by Charles Vildrac, the second (*The Kingdom of Sancho Panza*) by Melchior Lengyel. To the end of his life he was translating and adapting—not always to make money (though that was usually a consideration) but because, generally, he had made a discovery, and forthwith had to pass it on to others. "Have you read such and such?" he would ask. "Swell show. Needs some fixing. I think I'll do it for Hopkins [or some other manager] and if he doesn't want it, I don't care anyway. Swell show."

Again the Myers'. My wife and I were living way up under the roof in the ancient apartment known formerly as the Hotel de Ranes, 21 Rue Visconti, in a room rented to us by the Myers', who lived in an apartment on the second floor. The same winter Stephen and Rosemary Benet lived in a diminutive apartment in the courtyard, formerly, it is said, the stables where Racine had kept his horses. Alice Lee was Dick Myers' wife—and still is.

Books and plays and people, art, journalism and abstract ideas had their high and honored places in Sidney's scheme of things, but children always took precedence. His wires and letters of congratulation on the births of our three children were hardly perfunctory. Sidney couldn't do anything perfunctorily. The first of his three congratulatory messages is in the next long letter, but before I give you that I offer in evidence the wire that came to us shortly after the birth of our youngest in 1930. This was from Hollywood, early in March:

> Dear Clarks Love to both of you and all three of the rest of you and call the third something American Revolutionary to go with the first and second stop I suggest either Matthew or Israel Love Sidney.

The long letter from Geneva, printed below, was hurriedly typed on what must have been a rickety European machine. There are no paragraphs and the margins are narrow; and I know it was quickly typed. I have several such torrential outpourings—unpremeditated monologues. There are sentences and unfinished phrases in some of them I can no longer connect with anything I remember. Just a few points need clarification. My wife and I had been living in Berlin for about a year, and our first child was born there in August, 1923. We had been around a good deal with Sidney's mother in Paris the season before; we had seen her more recently in Berlin, and I had written telling her about the baby. What the "charming piece" of his own was I am not sure; it was probably *They Knew What They Wanted*. The Swiss banknote (fifty francs) was welcome indeed—we were living on seventy-five dollars a month. It bought clothes for the infant. The "Johnny" here mentioned was my childhood friend, Sanford Griffith, a brilliant young journalist, then representing the New York Herald in Berlin.

Sept. 18, 23. Dear old Barrett. When I passed through Paris the other day I dined with my mother and she told me about the baby. My dear man and also lady, this is pretty grand news. It is certainly the grandest news any two people can ever in their whole lives have to offer. My greetings and Clare's to all three of you and to the youngest in particular. I find myself on the brink of envying such as you because we haven't one yet. That approaches what people here call 'a frank statement.' Only that a frank statement here means the damnedest lie that the damnedest liar has the nerve to concoct. However, watch the Howards. There'll be a playmate for the young Clark yet. Perhaps a husband. Who knows? It must be years since I've written. Clare was ill pretty much all the first year we were married—the year terminated on the first of June last—and conditions in general kept me from a lot of things. But I am writing at last. You had to give me a real subject for the w.k. epistolary muse. Not that you haven't been particularly in my mind the last few weeks. I'll tell you why, or perhaps you know already. In Salzburg, in August—we went there on Reinhardt's invite to see *Le Malade imaginaire* acted just so perfectly and properly in that schloss of his—I met Von Hofmannsthal. He's a charmer and no mistake. And he met me entirely thanks to words spoken by yourself re the *Great World Theater*. The result is that I am to translate the thing for America where it will fail completely, but I am glad to have the chance and that grateful to you, as I need not say. . . . Now at that time I was headed for Prague, where I was to get from Masaryk a memoir for American serialization. This on order from Hapgood. Hofmannsthal was considerably exercised over the safety of the prompt book from which I am to work, and he agreed to send it to you. I planned, you see, to do my job in Prague and then to have a look at Germany and Berlin, in particular through your eyes and Cecile's—I never can spell her name and she must forgive me because I seem to hear the accents of the nefarious ———— [someone neither of us liked] saying Ceceele—and it would so have been easy and safe for me to pick it—the prompt book—up. Well, I got to Prague. Hapgood had been visiting Masaryk in the merrie month of May and failed to learn that he was then writing his own autobiography, although he must have been working ten hours a day on it. I didn't see myself in the role of the young reporter who says to him: Look here, you may be a president and the father of a country and a great social philosopher and all that, but you can't write up to the tastes of our readers. Our readers! So, after I had arranged to get Hapgood the refusal of the real thing, I sped out to the bank to get some money and send you a telegram announcing our arrival. We planned a few days in Dresden, then Berlin, then London. At the bank I found a cable for Clare from Mary Pickford ordering her to Hollywood a month earlier than we had expected. She is playing Queen Elizabeth opposite America's Sweetheart in a classix known to the vulgar as *Dorothy Vernon of Haddon Hall*. Result was one afternoon in Dresden and the schnellzug to London. There I found out about the League's [i.e., League of Nations] coming dope agitation and also that the assignment had been given to one Frazier Hunt who is a good man but for Anglophobia. Inasmuch as the dope agitation centers on a row between a damned fool episcopal bishop and the British India Office, I determined to save the Empire on my own account and come over here with Clare, an Anglomaniac, concurred so heartily that she went home alone. Again I got my eye on Berlin, thinking, three days Geneva, Munich, Berlin. Very nice and easy. See Clark familie and return to London to sail on the 29th. But now I know that that cannot be. I have more than enough to do here for the remainder of this week and I am already ordered back to London to write some more stuff there. So I am asking you to mail that prompt book, if it ever reached you, to me at Garland's Hotel, 16 Suffolk Street, Pall Mall. I don't feel so badly about you because my mother told me you are presently coming back to God's country. To Briarcliff? Or is the family estate there sold? It sounds like an ideal place for the Clark young. We are bursting into the country. Not to commute. That were too stiff for Clare. But we have now the top two floors and roof of a house on Lexington Avenue (969, to be exact) and we are supplementing that with a diminutive farm in Maine not far from

(197)

Clare's ancestors in Bath. It all listens quite well. I go back to rehearsals of *The Kingdom of Sancho Panza* in which Mr. Otis Skinner is about to tread the boards. . . . I have just finished a charming piece of my own. It really is rather charming. How soon are you coming home? Soon enough to split Von Hofmannsthal with me? Write me to London. The closing item is the enclosure. I thought of a present from Aunt Clare and Uncle Sidney to be purchased here and sent to Berlin. Then that seemed pretty seriously complicated, customs and all considered. So I did this. A check were better form—more delicate or something. This has a crass look. But Swiss francs are Swiss francs and will remain Swiss francs for some time to come in Germany. Therefore pardon the lack of delicacy, excuse my glove and all that, and give the young 'un a rattle or something she has seen in a shop window and wants, with love from both of us to all three of you. By the way, you will have a Communist uprising in Germany if Stresemann doesn't pull off his currency reform. Since my afternoon in Dresden I have founded a society to increase the per capita consumption of prussic acid among the French. I am still the only member but that is because it has to be a choosy society. Do you want to join? Or, Johnny, perhaps. Give him our best, too. Writing this has made me very lonely but I'm glad I did it. . . . I am serious about Von H.'s translation. My German is shaky and we might very well do it together. Let me know what you think of it—50–50, your dates, etc. And if you can get back soon enough for honest Morris Gest, I'll fix the contract.

It was only a few weeks after the date of this letter (November 1923) that we came home, and the following note was delivered the day after we re-opened the house:

I'm that sorry I'm not seeing you the moment you land. I shall be in New York again about December 7th for more work at the old stand. Bless you and Cecile and little Miss Clark. What a life! Again—Mr. Gest hasn't yet paid up or signed up because he is interested in *The Miracle* and in nothing else. I have written Sayler and had no answer.

When we landed in America I had no regular job and only a few prospects; but I did have a number of articles, which I was hoping to sell. Among these were a short intimate paper on Gorky, and a long impersonal pseudo-scientific report on conditions in Germany. I sent them both to Sid for advice. The first of his next two letters was from Washington, late in 1923 or early in 1924:

> I've read the German notes and I think decidedly that you can make something of them, though Hapgood might not see them in their present form. And frankly, I should be sorry to see them printed as they stand, for I think they lack sympathy to such an extent that they would really seem to stimulate the anti-German hatred from which the world is so cruelly suffering. No matter how realistic an article, how faithful its reporting, it requires an emotional objective and direction. Surely the decay of the German character is as pitiable as anything could well be. It is a decay far more disastrous than that of the South after the Civil War, and France after the final exile of Napoleon remained virtually unchastened and unrepentant. My own feeling toward Germany is, I think, kindlier than yours. I want some other things in this article and a friendlier direction. May I keep it until you come into town again? Bring any pictures you have and let me presume to give you a few suggestions—a lead—an ending on Bahr's statement of the cure. It seems to me a world obligation, now, to give the Germans a square deal plus the benefit of the doubt. And the thing ought to be printed for its grand stuff. Affection.

The second is on a letterhead with the 969 Lexington Avenue address:

> I should have written you sooner about the Gorky article, but I am down and out and far behind, having been ill and generally in distress. I think it good copy—very good—and a neat picture of the man. If you can make it better, fuller and timelier, do so. I don't hold with sending out copy, promising to improve if accepted. I'd try it and try marketing through B. and K.'s [i.e. Brandt & Kirkpatrick] new and very good article department.

I had intended to put in here several short notes, dating from the pre-*They Knew What They Wanted* years, but most of them would be meaningless without long commentaries that would take up more space than the letters themselves. One of these urges me to see Dudly Digges and Augustin Duncan who may be interested in my version of a new play Gorky had given me to adapt and sell ("Equity might give you Duncan"); one expresses the hope that I might be able to get a copy of *Swords* into the hands of Richard Strauss, whom I'd met in Berlin (nothing came of that); one whimsically describes a spell of sickness ("I've been a bit 'poorly' as they say in New England"); another asked me to inquire of our friend Alfred Goldsmith, the bookman, if he has a *Jurgen* "first" that is not too expensive: "I have a pretty thought which is to send it to Cabell for an autograph inscribing it to Scott Fitzgerald who had dernièrement become rather a buddy of mine."

But the later missives are more revealing, and most of them need little explanation. The next one I am printing has to do with my short review of *They Knew What They Wanted*, and was written in the spring of 1924.

No description of Sid Howard would do him justice that left out his comments on the books and persons he disliked, or that failed to show him in moments of disgust or anger. I have of course no right to leave in these letters some of the unflattering strictures he passed on plays and writers, and I am sorry I cannot print them. However, I am at liberty to recall how (in 1922 or 1923) he and I, having taken St. John Ervine and his wife to lunch at the Algonquin, were engaged in a terribly earnest conversation over our coffee. Two strange figures came over to a table next to ours—one short and stout, the other tall and not so stout as he became later on. Without introducing themselves they spoke over Sidney's head and mine to our guests, and one of them (I think it was the taller) solemnly announced, "You'd better come over to our table when you're bored." It was perfectly clear to me that Messrs. Woollcott and Heywood Broun were in a facetious mood, but Sidney was mad through and through. The Ervines and I laughed, but Sidney was ready to fight.

Another time he had asked me to introduce him to ——, a fairly well-known playwright whose work he liked. The luncheon at the Harvard Club was a failure. I can't explain it, but every topic of conversation ended up some blind alley, and after a short time Sid just sat back in his chair, bit his lip and fidgetted with his moustache. Maybe it was because our guest hadn't wanted a cocktail. He got up and left early, and Sidney and I laughed. "There's a dumb cluck! Let's get our drinks now! I wonder who wrote his play for him?"

This last is characteristic, not of his occasional lack of sympathy with a man he didn't like, but of his quick reaction to a given situation. Another man we had both known did something that in my own way I resented and described to Sid as "not very decent." "Not very decent?" he snapped. "Barrett, our friend —— is just a plain son of a bitch." This expression, you will understand, was not so widely used in the 20's as it is today.

And now for the next letter:

> Thanks for your note and the grand notice you gave the play. As to cutting Joe, there you raise the most interesting point that has been raised yet. I did cut him a good deal because he tended to overbalance the others . . . which was not good because the play is really about Tony and Amy. I dare-say you agree to that, and I don't think that I cut anything of any value. I am inclined to think that the trouble may be in his being *too* actual. I knew the man and reported him over-faithfully and there were moments when I stuck so close to him that, odd as it may seem, he ceased to be theatric and became improbable. After all, the play is a little (and unimportant) treatise on the obsessions which make the world go round. The woman's obsession for security—the man's, for a dynasty—on the one hand (Tony) and for rebellion on the other (Joe's). It is always dangerous to stick too closely to an original and I may have got Joe into the trouble you find by just that process. Another thing is that Anders, admirable as his performance is, does not quite understand the inarticulate quality of his part—the groping . . . ideas. He often makes a

transition in Joe's mind sound like a cut. For myself, I like best in the play my medieval morality at the opening of the 3rd act, where capital, rebellion & the facts of the case—pragmatic church—are all worsted by the woman's knowledge of the day of the week. I'm boring you with all this because your review is the very best thing the play has had, the most searching and the most understanding. When Bob Benchley covered both *Desire Under the Elms* & *They Knew What They Wanted* as French triangles I was outraged for both O'Neill and myself. I'm delighted, too, at your review of *Desire*. There's a fine play! There's rather a showing, these days, for American plays, isn't there? There may not be any *great* ones —though Stallings & Anderson are pretty near—but there are four of them—doing big business and earning at least serious respect—and that's *not* bad. Isn't Pauline Lord a great actress? *Really* a great actress? She's had an awful effect on me. Every word I write seems absolutely flat. I hear her say 'let go of my skirt,' and I'm gone, absolutely gone for the day. I can't get her out of my mind. Love to Cecile from both of us. When do we eat again? . . . Wednesday (which is chicken and waffles day at the Coffee House) I do recommend. Affection.

These words about Pauline Lord came back to me (I hadn't thought of them for years) when I saw Miss Lord at Sidney's funeral; she stood motionless in the cemetery, with the air of having just arrived from nowhere at all, precisely as she did in the first act of *They Knew What They Wanted*. I realized then what Sidney meant.

The success of that play and of so many others that followed it brought the inevitable lawsuit for alleged plagiarism and the threat of another from persons who believed Sidney capable of stealing their ideas. I think that in both cases the plaintiffs were not the ordinary kind of snipers who file claim and hope for a settlement from an author who may be willing to pay a few hundred dollars to avoid the greater expense and worry of maintaining his innocence in court. I testified in the one case that came to trial and prepared testimony and reports for the other case, which was dropped when Sidney categorically assured the author he had never seen, read, or even heard of her play. I can't imagine how anyone, looking into his blue-gray eyes, could possibly imagine him capable of plagiarizing anything. On the title page of the MS of *The Rivet* he wrote my name boldly above his own, and if I had not insisted that that of the man who had done four-fifths of the work should stand first, it would so have remained; *Dodsworth*, to judge from the title page, would seem to be a hack job that Sidney did a little work on; and *Yellow Jack*, as "original" as any play I know, was announced as written "in collaboration with Paul de Kruif."

The next letter came from Wiscasset, Maine, I think in the summer of 1930:

> Specifically, I need in my plagiarism suit a play in which the wife takes a lover because her husband is an invalid. Anything in that direction will do. I have just read the ridiculous affair which I was accused of robbing and I can destroy it finally and forever—though it bears no resemblance to "They Knew What They Wanted"—if I can show that their story is not original. Their story—I retail it, because I am asking you for help—is briefly this. A Swiss guide and his bride come home from their wedding and find there a Chasseur Alpin vagabond who makes an immediate set for the lady. The husband is called out to rescue some mountain climbers who have fallen into a crevasse and himself falls and is brought home paralyzed. The Chasseur stays in the house to help while the bride nurses her husband for seven months and falls in love with the Chasseur (bad sentence, very.) The upshot is sex and the paralytic miraculously cured so that he can murder the lover and violate his wife, much against her will. That is the play which I want to prove is not at all original in plot, basic plot of course. Aside from the story, it is a pathetic effort which would play only about forty five minutes with all its big scenes. It has no characterization, reality or merit of any kind. But there is the accident motive. The differences are obvious between that play and mine. The wife in mine does not love her husband, has never seen him. Does not love her seducer. Has the mistaken identity theme. I have the baby motive. The plays have no real similarity of any kind. Even the accident, in their play,

occurs *after* the marriage. But I want to make assurance
doubly sure by discrediting the originality of their play. Or,
for that matter, of my own. But theirs, I think, is the easier to
discredit. I have, already, an Edith Wharton story. I want a
French play in which a wife, married to an invalid, turns to a
lover for consolation. Just that much is enough. Can you pro-
vide, Lord?

A few days later these two notes arrived:

The complaint says: '. . . the unique portion of the tri-
angle being that the husband of the woman is incapacitated
from marital duties on his wedding night, thus giving the
other man a chance of pleading love for the woman while the
husband is helpless . . .' All of your examples, including *Le
Chemineau,* are valuable and germane as destroying the
uniqueness, still, if you think of one in which anything happens on the wedding night, I shall then be perfectly happy. I
can't believe that the smutty minded Frogs and the old Italian
comedy passed up anything as rich as that.

I feel sure now that the brief reference to so many plays
will clear all my difficulties away. I can say, granting the acci-
dental slight similarity which *They Knew What They Wanted*
bears to *The Full of the Moon,* allow me to show that *The Full
of the Moon* is not exactly an original composition. Bless you
for all your help. Now, one other thing. There was an old play
made from Mark Twain's famous character, Colonel Mul-
berry Sellers. I believe it was called *The Mighty Dollar.* One
John C. Raymond, a great comedian of the seventies, played
it. . . .I'm thinking there might be something in it. The
Colonel was a great old boy.

The trial, ably handled by Sidney's old friend and attorney Ernest Angell, was rather exciting. Until I was called
to the witness stand I sat with Clare Eames in the "audience,"
doing my best to keep her from interrupting the proceed-
ings. Sidney, when on the stand or sitting at the table with
Angell, cast anxious glances in our direction, while Clare muttered audible stage whispers. At one point in the argument of
the opposition she almost shouted, "What damn nonsense!",

and the Judge thumped his gavel, though he didn't seem to be much in earnest; he too was enjoying the show. I had prepared what we all thought was pretty good defense testimony in the shape of several plots from 15th and 16th century French farces. When I went on the stand Angell, looking very business-like and sharp, asked me to give the Judge, in brief form, a few examples of Gallic plots which would show that *They Knew What They Wanted*, if it was "stolen," was based on common literary property in existence centuries before the plaintiffs play was even thought of. Reduced to brief synopses, most of these sounded like short tales from *The Decameron*, and at one point I hesitated. Sidney smiled, and from the far end of the courtroom I could see Clare, her elbows on the bench in front of her, encouraging me to go ahead. She was grinning. After I had offered three or four examples the Judge told me that that was enough, and hinted jokingly that he might have to clear the court if I went on. The case was dismissed.

Not long after this a woman claimed that *The Silver Cord* had been taken from or inspired by a play of hers, but I have already told what happened in that case. I am inclined to believe that the characteristic preface to the book of *They Knew What They Wanted* was in effect a public invitation to obscure writers to sue Howard. "The story of this play," he wrote, "in its noblest form, served Richard Wagner as the libretto for the greatest of all romantic operas." And this very sentence was introduced in court as evidence of the thieving propensities of the man who wrote it. When confronted with the book, from which the attorney read the passage aloud, Sidney could hardly keep from snorting, while Clare held her handkerchief tight over her mouth.

Here are two notes that may serve as an interlude between the period of Sidney's first marriage, and the next decade that began with his second. Clare Eames, from whom he had been divorced some time before, died in London toward

the end of 1930; and early the following year he married Leopoldine ("Polly") Damrosch.

The first of these two notes was in answer to an invitation to come up to Columbia and let my class in dramatic
criticism (I was substituting then for Joseph Wood Krutch)
fire questions at him. I knew he would react quickly and de-
cisively; if the idea had appealed to him he might think it fun
to bring up half a dozen dramatists and spend the day arguing; on the other hand—well, this is what he wrote, on a large
sheet of expensive-looking bond paper:

Dear Barrett:
    Jesus, no!!
        Affection.

It wasn't even signed.
    The next note—from Maine—reads:

> Can you arrange to lunch with me on Friday? I am com-
> ing to town for Thursday and Friday to see Jed Harris and I
> want very much to discuss something with you, something, I
> hastened to add, which will give you a great deal of work but
> from which I expect to derive great benefit.

This is curious. He either intended to insert the word "you"
after the phrase "I expect," or else he wrote the whole thing
with an imagined stage direction—(*smiles*)—between the
lines. Just what it was he wanted of me I'm not sure; it may
have been the notion he once had of paying me to read each of
of his MSS as he finished it, in its first form, and fire back my red-
hot impressions of it. I know he wanted such reactions, and he
got them, from his friend and agent Harold Freedman, from
Clare Eames, and later from Polly, his second wife; and no
doubt from others. Of course, I laughed off his offer to pay me,
but I know now that one reason he always sent Christmas
presents to the children was his queer sense of obligation to
me. Yet he would have remembered the youngsters anyway.
He always bought these presents himself, and he usually

turned up at my office loaded with packages just before Christmas. Once he barged in and, surrounded by customers, ripped open a large package from which he extracted, piece by piece, a complete doll's washing outfit, laying the ironing board and clothespins and tiny electric irons on a long table, the strangers looking on in astonishment. One of them told me afterwards that he had taken the tall handsome visitor to be a toy salesman!—"D'ye think Molly will like that?" Sidney boomed. Next he unfolded an Indian costume and pushing me into the hallway began shooting arrows at a target. "Will the kid like this? You haven't any damn silly theory about not giving him lethal weapons, have you?

I read most of his plays in their first drafts, and sent back long criticisms of them. He rarely acknowledged these letters, because he claimed that adverse criticism—while he valued and wanted it—hurt his feelings at the time. He especially wanted Cecile's judgment on *Alien Corn,* because in that play he was chiefly concerned with the psychology of a talented young woman pianist. My wife's reaction was the same as mine: the play didn't ring true. We sent him a long report. Silence. A week later I met him on Fifth Avenue, and he was ill at ease. He blushed and said "You and Cecile didn't like my show, did you. I'm cutting a hell of a lot from it." And that was all, but our criticism rankled, and when, after the play was produced in 1933 he sent me a copy of the published book, he wrote in it, "As I look back on our conversation about first editions last night (on our way to see *Little Ol' Boy*) I feel that I ought to inscribe this one to you (a) because you never liked this play and (b) because it will be worth much less in the years [to come] than it is now."

I have already told something of Sidney's reactions to my criticism of the early drafts of his plays. If he disliked, for the time being, most kinds of adverse criticism, he nevertheless listened to it, knowing that some of it might be helpful; and how grateful he was—as will be seen from several of these letters—for any evidence of appreciation, particularly if it applied to something that was not obvious to other persons! The next letter was written at his sister's home in Berkeley, California. The date is June, 1929:

> Two letters of yours sit here unanswered and have been sitting these past I don't know how many days that I have been writing so hard. One of them asks if you can do something about foreign rights on *They Knew What They Wanted.* Of course you can if you care to lose money on the postage. Why don't you buy the amateur rights to the piece? It does very well by amateurs. In Santa Barbara they got the local fish man in to play it and he was a triumph. In Dallas the other day it won a prize. The other letter is harder to answer. I shall pause, now, light my pipe and read it again. I have read it again. Since I wrote you I have spent a blissful month on a play called *Half Gods,* in which I am trying to get down some of American womanhood's revolt against marriage, kidded of course, but still pretty much as I see it. I don't know that it is going to be much of a play. I never have had that feeling of writing a masterpiece. The excitement lasts while I am working and wears off into nothing, not even depression. But I do know that I have had a swell time of it and that I am beginning to be able to work again after what seems to me an interminable time. I don't believe that I shall give up writing for the theater until the theater gives me up. That is to say: I have got through with melodrama, with reporting and even with the strong story play. I think I am interested, now, in trying to dramatize what these people of ours are thinking about, not in a critical sense, but as it is, heightened by some kind of intensification that comes automatically with dramatic condensing. I am eager to go ahead with four plays and eager to get on to a novel. I dread my impending return to Hollywood. I dread it so that I have a strong feeling that I shall, somehow, try to back out if I possibly can. I see my daughter [Jennifer] though, as a more important job than any number of plays that *I* can write and I have to get back or do something which makes big dough to ensure my custody of her. I have got *Half Gods* a little better than half done and the worst scenes, except the final one, are licked. About August first I shall ship it off to you to read and

stamp upon or like or whatever. I can't get off my track even if I had some exalted vision of my talents and wanted to do so, because I am and shall always be an earthbound pragmatic stoic without any aptitude for the empyrean. I have had a bad time for two years. If I can still write for the theater without Clare's invaluable advice and guidance, I shall certainly go on writing for the theater. The above, with love to you both or, rather, all four of you, is the safest permanent address.

We were both delighted with *Half Gods,* and we thought the half-symbolical farce scene ("Keystone Comedy") one of the best in the show. My letter of comment was acknowledged in the following from Hollywood, in September:

Your letter did me no end of good because it said what I wanted to hear about my Keystone Comedy scene. I've had rather a time trying to dramatize the rest of the play with everybody (except my own Laura Crews) telling me how lousy that scene is. It was the only thing I was sure of in the play. The whole thing is now taking shape and feeling and has been growing from day to day since I sent that script you read off to be typed. I always get didactic passages in and then, by slow degrees, get them dramatized out. I think the play will be characters before I'm done. For instance, the psychoanalyst scene which I balled up badly will be one long piece of horseplay at the expense of those gents and, I trust, very funny in the way it leads Hope further and further from the straight and narrow. I'm plugging away in the few hours I can steal from the pictures. Thank God they are over in a few days more. I shall be East soon after the first of the month. I shall ask you to read the manuscript as revised and to talk to me about that. I shouldn't have sent that script out, I know, but I had Goldwyn calling me back here, and there was no chance, at the moment, of the month more I needed to work in peace. In the meanwhile bless you for your kind words which I needed badly when they came an hour ago.

One more "interlude" letter and a wire before I introduce the later series; I take only a phrase from the letter, written in the spring of 1919 from Hollywood:

I'll write you a lot I have on my mind soon. I've been

busy, bored, lonely and interested for five months. Now I'm going to my sister's to write plays.

I don't know precisely where this next wire belongs, but I believe it should go here. One day, it was probably in the early thirties, Sid breezed into my office and told me he was on his way to Iowa to investigate the farm situation and talk with some of my university friends whose dramatic productions I thought were worth looking at. "I want to see your friend Mabie at Iowa State U.—and I want him to put me in touch with some of the farm people. Give me your other names. Anyone in the Dakotas? *Bon!* Thanks. You'll hear from me. So-long!" And he strode out, his coat pockets stuffed with papers and magazines.

Four days afterward, he sent this wire from Des Moines:

> Dear Barrett Finishing my cruise with visit to A. G. Arvold of Fargo North Dakota stop If you have connections with him should appreciate your wiring him that I am pleasant sort of chap stop Mabie and setup are great affection Sidney.

Either just before this wire came, or just after, Sid called me long distance to tell about his "great trip," the "swell time" he was having, and what a "grand play" he was going to write about the Iowa farmers' strikes.

Though the next letter, written a few days afterward, was in answer to questions asked in connection with a little book I was writing on recent American drama, it got Sid started; he was in a mental state that plainly shows him working out of one of his depressed moods. Such moods were not uncommon, and even during the earliest years he would every so often swear he was done with the theater forever. "It's too unsatisfactory," is how he put it. "You get all steamed up over a play, and by the time it reaches the stage you go stale. No more plays for me—I'm going to do novels and stories from now on." And then, after a few days or weeks, he would write

—if he was away—or tell me if I was with him, about his "gorgeous idea" for a new show. "You'll like this one. It's all about ——."

Letters like yours are terribly hard to answer. The general dope and facts and dates are all in *Who's Who,* I expect, so we can omit them. I don't know what urged me to write. I grew up in a mess of books. My father was a self-educated man. There is a story, I think true, that he began his education working in a second-hand book shop after the hours he spent working on the wharves of the Philadelphia and Reading in Philadelphia. He was twelve then. He was what is called a "great reader." I inherited two of his three enthusiasms. I inherited books and gardening. His third and greatest enthusiasm, science, skipped me except that I have a kind of curiosity about people rather than rocks and plants. I began writing poetry pretty early in life. I think that I always fumbled around for some kind of artistic expression. I liked music better than anything and always raged because I wasn't able to get ahead with it. I gave it up, like a fool. I could have great fun, now, if I were able to play a piano even badly. I grew up in California. I was next to the youngest of six of which one sister was the oldest. I went to public schools and read books and camped in the high Sierras and rode horses and went to British Columbia and Mexico. I was taken to Italy when I was seventeen. I was sickly a good deal as a kid and never did well at sports. That's always given me a complex. My father discouraged my wanting to write. I know that he would have liked having a writer son more than anything, but his standards were high. He would think very little of my talents, I may tell you. And he would be quite right about them. Once he gave me an edition of Ibsen which I very much wanted and added that I was to wash the taste out with a good draught of Huxley. Young Raimund von Hofmannsthal has just blown in and out to say goodby, as he starts from here for Vienna via Java and points east and thinks that if he could get a great novel written on the way his father might be kinder to him. He is hurrying home to be there for his twenty-third birthday. He takes me back rather. We hadn't much of any money in our family but a sound example of hard work. Oh, and a great deal of music. Both my father and mother were pretty fair musicians. My mother had long earned her living as a professional, an organist and a piano teacher. Quite successfully. My father was a Handel hound. We had to learn Handel choruses as kids and keep time. On both sides we were pioneer stock. My mother's family came across the continent before '49. My father opened the first steamship line to Alaska. My grandfather opened Oregon and Washington by putting the first boats on the Columbia River. I can't remember very well how I first got interested in the theater. I just was, somehow, for no very good reason. Oh, yes, I had a toy theater, but then I had a toy everything else. I wrote plays in college when I went to California and was rather talked into going to the 47 Workshop course. I didn't like that, in which I was wrong and I have since eaten my words against it. I came very much under the influence of Sam Hume and his first new stagecraft show. But I chucked any idea of the theater to go over to drive an ambulance in France. Later, much later, when I was working, after the war, for *Life* and *Collier's Weekly* and doing labor investigating in the period when I first knew you well I translated D'Annunzio's *Fedra* for Nazimova, and Hume again. That got me interested again and *The Rivet* came along. In time Vildrac's *Tenacity* started me into an alley where I could function somehow for the theater, and there I've been since. Always about to tumble out into a world I like better than the theater and always picked up and put back. Clare held me hard to the theater, of course. I don't at all know what will happen to me now that Clare's let go. I'm in for this here for the present excepting some time this summer when I shall write some plays, but my heart seems to have gone out of that kind of writing and hasn't yet got fixed in any other kind. I am marking time for the moment, not liking it but being well paid and so not complaining. I always need some one with a club, and at the moment there isn't any one. I never acted and never wanted to. I am torn between the West where I belong biologically, if you know what I mean, and the East where I am not bored as I am in the West. I miss orchestras in the West, and people, and being near Europe. I've always been lonely and rather unpopular. Dass, aber, macht nichts aus. I have the hell of a conscience but don't do well at abstractions. Not at all well. In the philosophic sense, I mean. I have a vague plan, now, which includes saving money here . . . and working for some time

on a novel or two. I should think that I might presumably
drop out of the theater altogether, simply because there isn't
anything much to hold me to it and there is so much about it
that I find intensely uncongenial. That, I guess, comes from
shyness. There are so many close personal contacts in the theater. I don't function well with so many. I've liked one thing out
here. I've been so much left alone, which I like awfully. I am
going from here to the world's most beautiful garden (my sister's) where my young daughter is now waiting for me. There
I shall finish my Yellow Fever play and a comedy about marriage and a tragedy about the conflict between the artist and
the amateur. You'll read and see them both in due time. I discussed all that with you a year ago but it's been two years that
I haven't been able to write, because I couldn't get adjusted
to the break in my life and peace of mind. I'm O. K. now. Is
this hooey of any value at all?

A couple of days later a note came saying that "a long
wallop" of a letter had been sent me, "a fine picture of one
who knows not what he wants nor where he is. However,
things will come straight. They always do." The moody passages from 1930 and '31 on became less frequent (so far as they
are reflected in the letters), the plans for new plays more nu-
merous and elaborate; at the same time his interest in young
playwrights broadened and deepened and became more practical. I would often send him MSS to read, or urge him to attend try-outs of works by unknowns, friends or clients of mine
when I was in the agency business. In the following pages you
will read passages, for instance, about Lynn Riggs and his
early work; but I know that Sidney gave encouragement to
(which also usually meant got jobs for) many other youngsters
besides. The moment he read or saw a promising play he
would inevitably ask something like this: "Has the boy got a
job?—I want to see him.—He's got real talent. Would he go to
the Coast for a while?" And action followed. And I know he
helped young directors as well as managers. Though what I
am telling here and allowing Sidney to tell through his letters
is chiefly what I know from first-hand knowledge, I'm going to

quote a few lines from a letter Mike Blankfort wrote me soon after Sidney's death:

> I just met [him] after I directed Stevedore. He dropped me a note and asked me to have lunch with him at the Harvard Club. I wasn't anybody in particular and when he saw me and praised my job with the extravagance that was essentially his, and then abruptly changed the subject and asked in a voice that rang clamorously through the bar, 'What did I think of the Revolutionary Movement?' I sensed in all the thrill of being with him a strange, passionate, unafraid man. . . . I remember having a committee meeting with him on Dramatists' Guild business. Luise was there, perhaps you, Martin Flavin, and others. I asked permission to leave early. 'Why?' 'My wife's in the hospital,' I replied, 'she's having a baby.' Instantly the business of the meeting was over. Sidney and Martin and the others concentrated on advice: 'Who's the obstetrician? How long the labor? What hospital?' He took me to the hospital in a cab, stopping off at Brentano's to get a book for my wife whom he had never met; and when the baby came he sent her a beautiful gold locket.

Mike needed money and when he was in Hollywood he ran into Sid one day by chance.

> For six months I couldn't get a job. . . . Sidney came to town. His first words were, 'For God's sake, Mike, I hope the hell you haven't come out here to work for the movies!' . . . Within one afternoon three studios called me for work. It was his word to them. He had spent the afternoon on my behalf. . . . Somehow I feel that his death means more of a loss to the younger men than even to his own generation.

Sid's next letter was written from Beverly Hills, on a Samuel Goldwyn letterhead, in May 1930:

> I shan't be through here until the ninth of June. I shall come East some time in July. However, I won't be able to have a script finished by that time. I am sailing for France in July with the idea of taking a short holiday and at present plan to stay until I've finished a play for the Guild. It will be *Yellow Jack* and another, as *Yellow Jack* is almost completed. I have

been meaning to write you to thank you for the books you sent me and the dress for Jennifer, which is lovely and her very favorite. I was much interested in Mr. Geddes' plays. I wish that I had been able to deliver the play script earlier, but my work here has been too confining to permit of any serious writing. The Guild will be thoroughly bored with this further delay. I can only assure you that I will make every possible effort to submit a good play to them in time at least for a late production next season—say January.

I was at that time play reader for the Theater Guild, and hounding Sidney for his new play. The "Mr. Geddes" is Virgil Geddes, two of whose plays I had recently managed to get published. This note—left at my office the last day of July—shows that I didn't see him before he went abroad.

I got away from the theater and blew in on the chance of finding you. I sail tomorow on the Ile de France and don't come back until I've finished a play. If you feel like a whiskey and soda late this afternoon call me up at the University Club. Love to the family.

The next letter is from Santa Barbara (February 18, 1931):

I tried to see you in New York. The few minutes I had free always found you out. How perfectly fine about Lynn's play; it is really exciting news. I was so sorry when *Roadside* went badly. . . . I feel a little responsible for that too; I rooted so hard for Hopkins to Lynn. The news of me is brief and to the point: I am hard at work on *Alien Corn* and though it is still in a very crude state, believe hard in it and think that we shall have something to think about very shortly. Though I am not going to send it to the Guild until it seems really in shape. I hope they like it and want to do it. What is the news of you and what is Lynn's address? I mean Riggs, not Fontane. Who gets the Pulitzer Prize, Lynn or Phil? . . . I thought of you yesterday in Hollywood when I heard King Vidor say he plans to produce *Street Scene* as a picture. With Rice to cooperate Vidor might even make a good thing of it. I seem to have to do one more picture this spring, but shall not start it until

Alien Corn is finished, and possibly not until *Yellow Jack* is finished likewise. I have been offered plenty of work but none of it interests me in spite of the dough. I have good plans and really feel that I have never worked better. In fact, life looks awfully well at the moment. How are Cecile and the young? We are here until the middle of July. Are you too bored with me to write? What about this three-nighter Gene has done? If you can't say it between dinner and supper, put it in a novel. I mean that and go on record as opposed to bigger and better Hardys, Goethes and Methuselahs. With Wagner still in the lead, Gene's still got two nights to go to win out. No, *The Perils of Pauline* went longer. I suppose Wagner's music will be claimed as an unfair advantage. I am trying to get shorter and shorter. Charlie Chaplin's film being silent is tearing Hollywood asunder. Laura Hope Crews told me yesterday that its silence makes it of the past; Sam Goldwyn, given to enthusiasm but being an old hand, tells me it is of the future; tells me also that he is convinced talking pictures cannot succeed except in terms of melodrama, illustrating from his disappointment in Lonsdale's failure to go over big for Colman. This is interesting to me—and should be to you—because, as I must have told you long ago, it has been my conviction from the start of talking pictures. I think there is no doubt that they will slide into their place and become a bigger and better silent picture to fill the gap left by the old popular melodrama. As far as I can see, their only danger is in taking our people away and managers will simply have to revive the old art of writing contracts with their authors. You and I must get together hard on my new script, whether the Guild takes it or not. Wish to God that I had you here!

"Phil" is Philip Barry; and "Gene" Eugene O'Neill. The "three nighter" was subsequently reduced to the none too slender present form of *Mourning Becomes Electra*.

Your quandary about the Theater Guild is readily understood and your question about *Alien Corn* will be answered by my submitting the script to you unfinished for your criticism and at least a month before it goes to the Board. On the basis of that I should think that you could talk or look sour as you please. I mean, the Guild part of you, Pooh Bah that you are. Thanks a lot for Lynn's and the Glaspell plays.

I haven't had a moment to read 'em yet on account income tax, but Polly and I go off to Death Valley for a few days next week and they go along. A swell note from Lynn.

From this letter I judge that the Theater Guild Board had been after me to get hold of the first version of *Alien Corn*. The next letter (from Santa Barbara, March, 1931) shows Sidney at work finally on an idea he had had in mind for years: he had always been a Woodrow Wilson worshipper and wanted to "pin down" Wilson on paper.

Last fall in Vienna I decided to write a play about the Peace Conference at Versailles. My scheme, which is an ironic tragedy, excites me more deeply than any idea for writing that has ever crossed my mind. I shan't bore you with details though I am certain of your liking the idea. I am preparing for it with my head in a shelf of books some hours daily. I have discussed it with no one and I ask you to keep it to yourself. Last December I read in the Times about a play on Wilson by Emil Ludwig. It sounded in its resume like propaganda for the League of Nations. As such it caused me little if any uneasiness and I am so keen on my own scheme that I believe I should go ahead in the teeth of Shakespeare. I have recently, however, seen photographs of the Berlin production, in the Illustrated London News. Evidently the play has made more impression that I should have anticipated. You will undoubtedly have read it. What is it like and is the Guild considering it? I plan to get my reading done while I am here and to write my play next autumn in or near New York. I shall have to work in the East because I shall require help from experts here and there. This is for your information and, as I say, is confidential. I've discussed it only by letter with Norman Hapgood whose advice I needed to find how far I could go in manhandling the American political parties at the end which, I may tell you to whet your appetite, takes place at Boise Penrose's death bed.

The moment this letter came I decided to tell Theresa Helburn, because I didn't want the Guild to buy the Ludwig play if there was any chance of getting a Howard play on the same subject. I wrote Sid telling him what I had done.

Thank you for your letter about the Ludwig play. I don't know that I mind your having spoken to Terry. I should undoubtedly have done so myself but that I have promised so much and delivered so little of recent years. Too much promising makes one sound improbable. The Guild will not pass up Ludwig for Howard if it likes Ludwig, however, and I don't see that any harm is done by Terry's knowing all. Since you have gone so far and since I have already said so much, I may as well submit a night letter more about my scheme. I aim at the ironic tragedy of the defeat of the Wilson idea that a great nation in the heyday of its power might dedicate itself to the service rather than to the conquest of humanity. This, I believe, was what caught the world's attention when the war ended and made Wilson the figure he was at that time. This certainly was what Wilson believed the American people to be capable of and this, just as certainly, was what, for various reasons, the American people fell down on. Is such idealism beyond the spiritual strength of any people, one asks and the answer is probably yes. Not, however, that idealism per se is beyond a people, but that anything abstracted is beyond. The idea that we think with our memories and speak in phrases but act as usual according to the scattered patterns of our individual lives and the example of men with the force to lead us in ways which we can follow without thinking at all. I grow diffuse. Excuse, please. I think I know what I mean. I want to tell the story of Wilson's stand for open covenants openly arrived at because that stand seems to contain all the others and to be the most promising of dramatic material. There is, for point to the play and immediacy to the American public, an ironic analogy to be drawn between the secret connivings of the old European diplomacy and the secret connivings of the old American politics. Wilson set out to defeat the one and was destroyed by the other. By his unwillingness to meet the other, his determination, once he had taken his most lofty position, to defy it. I want, for example, to begin with that most moving interview which actually took place between Wilson and Frank Cobb of the World on the eve of Wilson's message to Congress in which he asked for the declaration of war as nobly as man ever asked for anything and in what seems the most striking of all the expressions of his ideal for America's service. The European diplomats and the American politicians furnish the body of the play with a goldmine of dramatic obstacles to place in the path of the central figure. I want to end at Boise Penrose's bedside when the telephone brought from Chicago the cheers which greeted Harding's nomination and the resignation of the old order in politics on this side of the Atlantic. Thus, the American aspect of my play is quite as important as the European or international and Ludwig is not likely to tackle that or even to understand or be interested in it. His play sounds to me like his usual genius worship plus a big blurb for life beside the Lake of Geneva. I don't think that is the way to handle Wilson. He was not a hero. He was a great idea, an idea worthy of godhead (with which he clearly thought himself endowed) tacked on to the personality of a Gregers Werle, and Ibsen ought to be writing about him, not Ludwig or me. If my play *Yellow Jack* turns out to suit me, I shall do Wilson in that same abstracted, pseu-do-chinese technic of acting and production about which I am so excited. I have, for the present, to finish work in hand and get ahead with my Peace Conference reading and shall hardly begin writing on Wilson before October. I'll be interested, of course, to hear anything more about the Ludwig play that you care to tell me and to consider your advice if you think that I am invading his field. But that last seems so unlikely to me that for the moment, I do not contemplate holding off. I ought to be able to get my play done by somebody. If only it weren't for debts ... and I have to take time out this summer to write and shoot two pictures. Thus, the best I can do before I come back in September is *Alien Corn* and *Yellow Jack* both finished and pray God to somebody's satisfaction. *Alien Corn* is drawing nicely to a close and should start on its way East very shortly. After that, I believe that I shall be finished with shooting for realism, at least for some time to come. I am further engaged in knocking out a synopsis for a heroic farce which opens with a young couple who murder their cook because they can get no other satisfaction against her and other members of the servant class and who eventually find themselves made a test case for civilization with the Deity as judge and Lenin as pros-ecuting attorney. The late Lenin. Only I'm tired of saying how full of ideas I am and, as I said above, not delivering. Last week I took four days out to drive to and about Death Valley and found it unimaginably magnificent and remote. There is this point to life in the West: you can take three days off, or four or five, or even one, and use them to go to some part which blows your head off and returns it to you dry cleaned and improved. You can't do that or get that effect from a week end of rest in Atlantic City, even with the gin in the suit-case. Life is quite fine. I got back from Death Valley to a children's party for Jennifer's birthday and survived even that.

The last of the letters on the Versailles play was a note from Santa Barbara, April 31:

Thanks for the lowdown. I think that if God himself were sitting on Ludwig's right I should still go ahead, though I haven't yet taken time to read *Versailles*. This is hastily dictated between the last gasps of *Alien Corn* and the first of a terrible but profitable picture.

This next belongs nowhere in particular, and might, for the sentiment it expresses, make its periodical appearance on every page. It is a wire from Topeka, and the date is December 23, 1929:

Dear Barrett Things got so crowded could not reach you Bid you Cecile goodbye have instructed University Club return Riggs play your office A doll goes to Molly and a necklace to Nancy from Santa Claus or me according to their education along those lines Merry Christmas.

The necklace is today Nancy's most precious possession, and the doll—christened Sidney the moment it was taken out of the box—is still alive, and Molly's favorite.

The "plan" spoken of in the next letter was one of many variations on the same theme I had conceived and tried to work out, attempts to persuade the professional managers and playwrights to give serious thought to the really important work being done in the best of our Little Theaters, colleges and universities. It was a rather ingenious plan, I think, involving production of new plays by established writers at various focal points throughout the country, and the statements I brought together and published were by no means perfunctory puffs. O'Neill, Hopkins, Green, Riggs, and Howard were my spiritual backers. The next letter was sent from the 82nd Street house in New York, March 1932:

> I read your piece with interest and admiration. Lynn came yesterday to talk at greater length about the plan and about what the Hedgerow people are doing for him. I naturally conclude that your tongue must be hanging out to hear what I think of it all. Need I say more than that I don't see how the younger playwrights are possibly going to get anywhere without it? What you are offering Lynn & Co. is what the Provincetown outfit offers O'Neill with the addition of the personal note which, had he had it, might have learned him to be less improving about Aeschylus. Your scheme, too, comes most happily in these days of Broadway bankruptcy. The youngsters are clearly going to have a harder and harder time, particularly those, like Lynn, who have a fresh way in dramatic story-telling. I clear my throat and proceed. Everything I see about me now seems passé in the most jaded sense, producers, critics, audience. Thursday afternoon the Metropolitan gave *Götterdämmerung* the most lofty and thrilling performance I have ever seen of Wagner, and who, but Howard and the standees, gave a damn. Snobbish remark, that. Broadway actors are jaded. Any freshness that appears among them is promptly swallowed by Hollywood. To free the playwright of this atmosphere is certainly to benefit the good health of playwriting. The country needs other lying-in wards than Broadway. The alleged native drama is going to become a great deal more native when it sees the light and takes its first steps in hardier neighborhoods and under a more selfless tradition. Lynn's superb new play perfectly demonstrates the rightness of your scheme . . . Jasper Deeter. Such men as he are the white hopes, and I am inclined to think that the best of them will offer the young writers something more than any of us had on either 36th (or was it 35th) or McDougal Street. Let me know if I can write, say or do anything to further matters. I am going West in a few days to make one more picture. *One* more? Well, another. I should be so glad to talk with Gilmor Brown.

Deeter was, and still is, director of the Hedgerow Theater at

Moylan-Rose Valley, Pa. He produced at least six of Lynn's plays. Gilmor Brown directs the Pasadena Playhouse. The next is the last communication I find on this subject. It came from Los Angeles, and was sent April 4, 1932:

> I wrote you in that letter just what I thought. If I were to add anything it would be this. The theater cannot enjoy its proper lease on life unless it is a part of the public's life. I am not one who feels that it is dying in New York, neither am I one who feels that New York is all of America. The great virtue of the Little Theaters and their value to the drama at large is that every Little Theater is a part of the life of its community. That seems to me the largest value of your scheme. Can't you knock a suitable statement out of my letter, taking care—because I don't remember what I wrote you—not to knock any of our struggling friends on Broadway; I think your statements are both fine. If I were to query one thing it would be your definition of the word "experimental." I don't know that I would use the word at all. It is so associated in the public's mind, as in my own, with plays which have not come off even according to their authors' vision of them. There is to my mind nothing experimental, for example, about Riggs' magnificent *Cherokee Night,* and the point is—isn't it?—that managers are apt nowadays to be afraid to take a chance on themes and departures which have not been tested.

From 1932 on, except for two or three long letters, my file offers only short notes: a sentence or a paragraph here and there shows concern over what the children want for Christmas; "How is Lynn getting on?"; "Tell Bein when you see him that I never heard from the Guggenheim people"; he had just seen Sherwood Anderson in Washington and "we both have vaguely the same idea for a play—a comedy to kid the radicals"; and how sorry he was I had to look over the proofs of his *Paths of Glory* for him. ("I still like that play").

But here is one short note I'd like to add; it is on Goldwyn stationery, from California. It came in January 1936:

> . . . When I read *Cherokee Night* I thought it a most poetic and original manifestation of this country of ours,

Riggs' best work and one of the truly fine things done by any American dramatist in our time. I have said as much to every manager I know. Now, as I sit here in Hollywood, thinking more in sorrow than in anger of the deadness of our New York stage I wonder why *The Cherokee Night* isn't put on the screen where—or so I am beginning to suspect—*Cherokee Night* and most other good things belong.

The next, coming so characteristically between "serious" discussions, but really more serious in his mind than plans for plays, came from Bar Harbor in June 1934:

> Thank you for the Shakespeare, which we are looking forward to eagerly. The text does not matter so long as it is all uniform, because I am putting the plays to a low use, namely, that of dividing up the parts among the kids, who then give daily dramatic readings, an act a day, between their supper and bedtime. Love to the family.

One December not so long ago he had not had time to do his Christmas shopping for the children. As the next letter shows, his conscience hurt him, and he mentioned the matter to me twice again during the following winter and spring. This is dated December 28, 1937:

> I should have written you sooner to answer your fine letter about *The Ghost of Yankee Doodle*. I am indeed pleased that Cecile and you liked the play. Your second letter comes this morning. I rather expect the play to close this coming Saturday night. Though it has been doing between eight and nine thousand a week with the subscription, the window sale would not justify expectations of half that figure now that the subscription is finished. . . . I got home from South America just in time to plunge into Christmas shopping, but not in time to get my Christmas shopping done with anything like completeness. I have betrayed the young Clarks' faith in me that I have built up through all these years. Or is there something they want that I can still provide between this morning of writing and my departure for Hollywood next Sunday?

The last long letters I have about plays (which I am running together) are the two that follow, February 5 and 18, 1938. Sid had been given a hint for an American comedy, of which the basic idea was similar to that of the Quinteros' play, *The Women Have Their Way*. He had asked me in a wire to get in touch with Granville-Barker and the Quinteros' agent:

> I have long been fooling with the idea of writing a comedy about a Confederate historical society in a small town in the Old South. Conceive of such a group, native ladies and elderly gentlemen torn by the snobbery and nonsense of an endless altercation over the problems of establishing in which particular house Stonewall Jackson spent the night before the battle of ———. The play could in fact be called *The Natchez Campaign*. Into this community comes Mr. Herbert Marshall as a young attorney from New York, sent down to settle an estate which involves the bequest to the historical society of a great collection of relics and documents of the Civil War. At once the new Natchez campaign is started, all factions uniting to marry Marshall to the librarian of the historical society. I have been, ever since I started the screen play of *Gone With the Wind* (now, thank God, completed), considerably involved with various representatives of Southern patriotic societies and, believe me, the field is a rich one for another *Christopher Bean*. The question is, how do you advise going about doing business with the brothers Quintero? My play, if it comes off at all, will be a much better play than theirs. I want to use nothing of theirs but this idea of a town which has never permitted an eligible unmarried man to get away unmarried. Actually, I could write the play without a suspicion, even on the Quinteros' part, of plagiarism. The fact remains, however, that the key idea came to me from what Chodorov told me about *The Women Have Their Way*. . . . My notion involves rather an ethical indebtedness than any kind of plagiarism and any obligation would certainly be discharged ethically—and perhaps legally—by an acknowledgement to the effect that the germ of the idea came to me from a Quintero play. . . . [There follows here a discussion of the report that the Quintero brothers were killed by one side or the other in the Spanish Civil War, and Sidney was advised to take such a report with a grain of salt.] . . . For myself, I am willing to believe any horror of either side in a revolution. I might, I suppose, go ahead with my play. I shall certainly visit the Southland before I do so. At the same time I will do

well to see what truth can be learnt about the Quinteros or their heirs and make some proposition to them if any truth can be got at. To give you some idea of how far I should depart from the original my scheme involves a bequest to a Confederate historical society. The bequest consists in a house which contains valuable historical collections. The society in question has for its main raison d'etre the exploitation of a brief and very unimportant campaign supposedly conducted by Stonewall Jackson. When my final scene comes in which the New York lawyer persuades the girl to accept him, he has found in the bequest a document which proves beyond peradventure of a doubt that the Jackson in question was not Stonewall Jackson but a mere captain of no importance, whose initials happened to be S. W. Thus, if she does not accept his hand he is in a position to annihilate her beloved society and all its researches. It is with this very local club that he gets the girl.

Nothing ever came of this idea, nor of the plan for what he called his "Iowa farm play," nor the "show about a commonplace girl in which nothing happens," nor the opera on Cabell's *Jurgen*. At the time of his death, as we know, he was doing an adaptation for Gilbert Miller and a historical piece on Franklin. Neither of these was finished.

During the last four years I had seen a lot of Sidney, usually in the office at the Dramatists' Guild, and once at his country house at Tyringham, and we met frequently as members of the board of the Dramatists' Play Service, the result of a pet scheme of his which he had brought to life in the summer of 1936.

There can be no proper *Finis* to these letters, no artistically arranged culmination. The end of this man's correspondence, so far as these few samples are concerned, must be as abrupt as the shocking and sudden end to his life. But it is fitting, and typical, that after I had gone through my files I should find on my desk, at the office, together with a number of other unanswered letters, a short note, written about

a month before his death, asking me to help a German refugee
get a job—a hurried and nearly illegible scratch:

> Can you find time to talk to Mr. ——— about community
> theater possibilities. Affection, Sid —

INDEX

INDEX

Contents

Contents

Contents